Making Curriculum POP

Developing Literacies in All Content Areas

Pam Goble, Ed.D.
Ryan R. Goble, M.A.

Foreword by William Kist

free spirit
PUBLISHING®

Library of Congress Cataloging-in-Publication Data
Goble, Pam B., author.
    Making curriculum pop : developing literacies in all content areas / Pam B. Goble, Ed.D. and Ryan R. Goble, M.A.
        pages cm
    Includes bibliographical references and index.
    ISBN 978-1-63198-061-9 (pbk.)
1. Internet in education. 2. Digital media. 3. Reading (Secondary) 4. Content area reading. 5. Language arts—Correlation with content subjects. I. Goble, Ryan R. , author. II. Title.
    LB1044.87.G636 2015
    371.33'44678—dc23

                                                                    2015023587

Cover and interior design by Colleen Rollins
Edited by Kurt Austin

10 9 8 7 6 5 4 3 2 1
Printed in the United States of America

Free Spirit Publishing Inc.
6325 Sandburg Road, Suite 100
Golden Valley, MN 55427-3629
(612) 338-2068
help4kids@freespirit.com
www.freespirit.com

This book is dedicated to
Ruth and John,
who loved sharing stories

Chicago, Illinois, 1942
Photograph courtesy of Ruth Bocian

Contents

Chapter 5: Learning Experience Organizers (LEOs)   133

Digital Content
Customizable digital versions of all LEOs in Chapter 5
Appendix: LEOs Aligned to Standards

Digital content can be downloaded at **freespirit.com/mcp-forms**.
Use password **media8**.

LIST OF FIGURES

Foreword

William Kist, Kent State University, Ohio

I'll start by saying that I think that "Making Curriculum Pop" is one of the smartest, most clever titles and concepts that I've heard for describing a paradigm or template for learning. (It's right up there with "Mindblue"— another Goble creation!) "Making Curriculum Pop" as a concept is brilliant not only because it promotes the use of pop culture in K–12 classrooms, but because it promotes a culture of teaching and learning that emphasizes engagement, that emphasizes the pop! The title itself pops and is fun. And, to paraphrase Auntie Mame, "We need a little fun. Right this very minute!"

It is so refreshing to read an education text that speaks not only about the Common Core but also mentions documents that we rarely hear about—the National Arts Education Association's standards, for example, and the Capacities for Imaginative Thinking. The Capacities list starts by asking kids to "notice deeply." As the father of young children, I see that little kids notice deeply rather effortlessly. But before too long, the party's over for them and it's time only to care about "what do I have to do to get an A?"

But even before I had my own children, I knew about the transcendent power that the arts and popular culture have to engage kids and to cross the boundaries that we so artificially set up in schools. As I've written elsewhere, showing the film *The Kid* to my ninth-grade students at Hyre Junior High in Akron, Ohio, was a truly profound "teachable moment"—both for my students and for me. I remember standing in the dark watching as my students stared open-mouthed at the screen. I think some of them got a little teary when little Jackie Coogan was taken away from Charlie Chaplin. They asked for more, and my interest in the so-called "new" literacies came from this moment related to a silent film, more than from anything I've ever learned from a "tech tip." Serendipitously, while I was showing my students old movies and asking them to make their own grainy videos, the Internet crept into our lives, and before we knew it the act of reading and writing became about all kinds of forms of representation—not just words. The Gobles are in my camp—they come at a broad-based conception of text not so much via a digital pathway, but through the ancient gateway of the arts as a way of knowing. To continue my Angela Lansbury theme: "Tale as old as time . . . ."

But to be clear, this book is not only retro, it's also extremely relevant and grounded in the Gobles' real-world knowledge of the way schools work. They understand that we educators must exist in the real world of standards and standardized testing, and nothing in this book is out of step with current realities. It's just that, in addition to a world in which a PLC exists on every corner, this book proposes that we also have an artist-in-residence on every corner. And maybe an architect and a casting director and a cartographer, to name just a few other people standing on the corner. The Gobles effectively debunk the silo structure that has been so prevalent in institutionalized education yet demonstrate a system for operationalizing interdisciplinary studies within our subject-bound schools. They do this based not only on their real-world experiences but also on their wide knowledge of scholarship and great thinking about human learning that has gone before them, work that has not always really been operationalized or even acknowledged in our current K–12 structures. As you'll see, Pam and Ryan have drawn widely from Maxine Greene to Harvey Daniels and Mihaly Csikszentmihalyi, and from Daniel Pink to Jimi Hendrix to Linda Darling-Hammond. This truly is a book of greatest hits!

But as anybody who's taken Jazz 101 knows, there can't be freedom without structure. The famous ninth note in a jazz chord sounds "blue" simply because it tweaks the do-re-mi structure that we Westerners are used to. So Pam and Ryan don't leave us without our scales. The Learning Experience Organizer (LEO) structure gives any teacher a nice scaffold (to mix my metaphors) into this so-called new way of teaching. And what blew my mind was the beautifully curated list of resources you'll see in Chapter 4, resources spanning text types and subjects, and organized in a way I've never seen before. That chapter alone is worth the price of admission.

Ultimately, what I think you'll also pick up from reading this book is exactly what those of us who already know Pam and Ryan already know— they are good people and master teachers. We're fortunate that they have taken the time to write down their ideas for us to use. Now, I'm off to the movies. And the art museum. And the concert hall. And to the library. And to my social network. It will be fun.

William Kist

INTRODUCTION

You may notice that throughout this book we talk about developing a teaching practice that is meaningful, engaging, and fun. That is why we decided to name the book *Making Curriculum Pop*. The title has a double meaning: we embrace pop culture as an essential part of classroom study, and we also get excited about teaching when experiencing fun, joy, and the unexpected.

When your curriculum "pops," it becomes more efficient, effective, fun, and engaging. It's like a cool tie, a great pop song you didn't expect to hear on the radio, or a giant bubble being popped by a preschooler. Obviously, our classes don't feel like this every moment, on every day, but the goal of our work has been to discover content and develop practices that make this kind of learning more the norm than the exception.

The title also links to the Making Curriculum Pop (MC POP) social network (mcpopmb.ning.com). Ryan coined the phrase and launched the website when he was working as a teacher-coach and curriculum coordinator at a high school in the South Bronx in 2009. MC POP is a place where teachers from all over the world collaborate by sharing articles, ideas, and resources to make curriculum more connected and intriguing for students across the disciplines.

> While we usually associate *text* with print, it is a term designed to expand our definition of "things that can be read." The more texts students can critically and creatively examine and create, the more well equipped they will be to mindfully navigate our complex and textually rich world.

Around the same time the MC POP social network came into being, we began thinking about how to create universal and interdisciplinary tools that teachers not formally trained in media education could use comfortably with a variety of curricula. With this nonprint and interdisciplinary focus in mind, we began building on Harvey Daniels's literature circles practices.

In classes and conferences our early experiments were well received by our K–12 students and graduate students. As the work evolved we found ourselves developing the wide range of Learning Experience Organizers (LEOs) collected in Chapter 5 that made our classrooms pop in unexpected ways.

Like its social network namesake, we hope this book allows us to continue learning from and conversing with our teacher friends, students, and readers. We hope that the collaborative learning strategies built around LEOs illustrated in this book make *your* curriculum pop the same way they have for ours. We also hope you will reach out to us to share the experiences and modifications you make on our ideas to experience the same enjoyment in learning that we do.

But before we start popping, we want to briefly explore the term *text*, glance at the way diverse standards explore the broader concepts of text and literacies, and also clarify the concepts of cooperative and collaborative learning as they apply to the learning experiences this book is designed to support.

Text as a Term

We struggled with what term to use to describe our tool. We started with the idea of media circles, but we felt that this term might be too exclusive. We then played with the idea of pop circles or text circles, and we felt that those terms also lacked clarity. While all these terms were acceptable, we felt we could focus on the widest range of subject matter and texts by conceptualizing all of our "role sheets" as Learning Experience Organizers. These LEOs are a vehicle for teachers and students to collaborate to make curriculum pop.

While we usually associate *text* with print, it is a term designed to expand our definition of "things that can be read." Broadening our understanding of the term allows us to talk about texts such as sculptures, baseball cards, landscapes, body art, webpages, movies, comics, songs, buildings, photos, and ads.

Text evolved into its present meaning after the advent of mass media—starting with newspapers, followed by radio, television, and film—when academics and teachers theorized that we could "read" a radio show or a film using many of the same skills we use to read a book. Simultaneously, schools of education and K–12 schools shifted from talking about "reading and writing" to the broader concepts of "literacy," "new literacies," "multimodal literacies," and "multiliteracies." At the moment and in this book, we capture this idea using the broad term *literacies*.

With the advent of digital technologies, our concepts of literacy expanded further. According to a national survey by the Kaiser Family Foundation (2010), eight- to eighteen-year-olds use entertainment media seven-and-a-half hours a day—more than fifty-three hours a week. The number goes up to ten hours a day if one accounts for media multitasking. New communication modalities are being developed seemingly on a daily basis, and they require as many, if not more, literacies than we afford to the written word alone.

This is one of many data points that urge us toward literacies that allow us to "read" a world where one creates, communicates, and collaborates through a seemingly infinite range of texts. The ubiquity of nonprint text requires students and adults to comprehend, critique, and compose across a wide range of symbol systems. The more texts students can critically and creatively examine and create, the more well equipped they will be to mindfully navigate our complex and textually rich world.

The powerful idea of supporting literacies in our classrooms is built around teaching "modes of representation much broader than language alone . . . [that] differ according to culture and context, and have specific cognitive, cultural and social effects."[1] This theory points to a world of texts worthy of study. For those who continue to focus on more traditionally assessed texts like reading and writing, research on media texts (the most familiar nonprint texts) is valuable to note. Many researchers have found that, over time, students are able to transfer concepts from media texts like viewing, listening/looking for details, decoding symbols, using context clues, and identifying themes, arguments, and organizational structures into their understanding of traditional print texts.

Again, focusing on media and digital texts, the 2011 New Media Consortium Horizon Report is instructive. The report—a collaboration between the New Media Consortium, the Consortium for School Networking, and the International Society for Technology in Education—states that "digital media literacy continues its rise in importance as a key skill in every discipline and profession," especially teaching, but goes on to remark that "training in digital literacy skills and techniques is rare in teacher education . . ."[2] This type of training and broadened understandings of texts are crucial to allow for an expanded scope of teaching and learning.

The National Council of Teachers of English (NCTE) was clearly able to see this need for an expanded definition of literacy over eighty years ago when they created a Committee on Photoplay Appreciation in 1932 that published study guides for teachers around the use of film. Since that time, calls for wider understandings of different kinds of texts have only increased. At the turn of the century, the 21st Century Skills movement began articulating ideas around communicating and composing in multiple modalities. NCTE released position statements, including the 2003 Resolution on Composing with Nonprint Media and summary statements on multimodal literacy, and the National Council for the Social Studies issued a strong position statement in 2009 on the importance of media literacy.

Expanding Standards

Following these earlier statements, the national Common Core State Standards movement began to address some of the same concerns. The

1. Cope & Kalantzis, 2000, p. 5.
2. New Media Consortium, 2011.

Common Core State Standards (CCSS) for English Language Arts have begun to articulate a more wide-angle view of literacy as the ability to read, write, listen, and speak across media through anchor strands like the following:

In reading . . .
CCSS.ELA-LITERACY.CCRA.R.7
Integrate and evaluate content presented in diverse media and formats, including visually and quantitatively, as well as in words.

In writing . . .
CCSS.ELA-LITERACY.CCRA.W.6
Use technology, including the Internet, to produce and publish writing and to interact and collaborate with others.

CCSS.ELA-LITERACY.CCRA.W.8
Gather relevant information from multiple print and digital sources, assess the credibility and accuracy of each source, and integrate the information while avoiding plagiarism.

In speaking and listening . . .
CCSS.ELA-LITERACY.CCRA.SL.2
Integrate and evaluate information presented in diverse media and formats, including visually, quantitatively, and orally.

CCSS.ELA-LITERACY.CCRA.SL.5
Make strategic use of digital media and visual displays of data to express information and enhance understanding of presentations.

The National Council for the Social Studies' College, Career, and Civic Life (C3) Framework for Social Studies State Standards echoes the concerns of the national English language arts standards.

In the science, technology, engineering, and math (STEM) disciplines, the CCSS's Eight Mathematical Practices focus on goals such as "creating mathematical models" (graphs, equations, or infographics), "constructing arguments and critiques," and "reasoning abstractly." The Next Generation Science Standards' (NGSS) Science and Engineering Practices call for students to create representations through models, analyze and interpret data, engage in argument, construct explanations, and evaluate and communicate information. All these skills require students to analyze, critique, and ultimately engage with a wide range of texts.

In our eyes, the National Arts Education Association's standards are the most elegant of the bunch, asking students to connect, respond, perform/present/produce, and create. This leads to one of the better boutique standards, developed by Lincoln Center Education in New York City.

Their Capacities for Imaginative Thinking are clearly inspired by the work of their past philosopher-in-residence (and heir of John Dewey's intellectual legacy), Maxine Greene. These capacities are the closest reflection of the intent of this book, as they are profoundly interdisciplinary and they ask students to collaborate to:

- notice deeply
- embody
- pose questions
- identify patterns
- make connections
- empathize
- live with ambiguity
- create meaning
- take action
- reflect/assess

Outside of these pedagogical and policy documents, we know on a practical level that humanities teachers use primary sources, including photos, art, and maps, and STEM teachers use graphs, simulations, infographics, and images. These texts, however, generally remain secondary to the kinds of reading, writing, and memorizing of formulas and key terms required of students on most standardized tests.

All the standards we have mentioned incorporate these wider ideas about texts and literacy, but nontraditional texts often remain neglected in favor of the traditional literacies of reading and writing. We like to approach standards and standardization with both care and caution, as they are often used more for control than creativity, collaboration, and creation.

We recognize that many valuable educational goals are often articulated by standards and that they remain "currency of the realm." We get most excited when standards are used by students and teachers to expand curriculum to create richer and more engaging learning environments. But we rarely *start* our work with standards; instead, we ask, "what would make a rich learning experience?" This question leads us to create learning experiences that easily align with standards after the fact. To help you do the same, we have aligned all the LEOs in Chapter 5 to a wide range of standards in the Appendix available in the digital content (see page viii for how to access this content). We hope this allows you to focus on making your curriculum pop first, and aligning your learning experience with school, state, district, and national initiatives second.

Fortuitously, every major set of national standards speaks to our need to read, write, speak, listen, view, and represent in a variety of modalities. This book is an effort to put these articulations into practice, by helping educators creatively integrate broad literacies into dynamic and engaging teaching practices.

Collaborative and Cooperative Learning

We have also noticed a second challenge around developing meaningful, purpose-driven collaborative learning in classrooms. Many teachers practice group work in the most informal sense by asking students to "get in a group of four" and work on a task. While this can be effective in many situations, group work can often be more powerful if it crosses into the realm of practices labeled collaborative and/or cooperative learning.

The literature on cooperative and collaborative learning presents varied ways to look at both concepts. Many sources stress collaborative learning as a philosophy and an umbrella term for more student-centered and student-directed group learning. Cooperative learning is often characterized as more teacher driven, focused on equitable contributions while utilizing specific structures and roles.

Depending on how you use the LEOs, students' learning experiences may be more structured and cooperative or organic and collaborative. We hope you take advantage of this continuum of practices to suit your classroom needs at any given time. If you assign students' texts and LEOs with a specific standard or goal in mind, you would be using LEOs in a more structured, cooperative way, but if students select their own LEOs and/or select their own texts for more open-ended inquiry, you would be using the LEOs in a more collaborative structure.

While your work may be both collaborative and cooperative, we ultimately used the thinking articulated by Roger and David Johnson's research on the traits of successful cooperative learning and constructive collaboration as the framework for making curriculum pop with LEOs. Their research focused on developing structures that promote:

- face-to-face interaction
- positive interdependence
- individual accountability
- social skills
- group processing abilities[3]

---

3. Johnson & Johnson, 1999.

Similarly, Kagan and Kagan also suggest that cooperative learning is successful because of four constructs:

- ○ positive interdependence
- ○ individual accountability
- ○ equal participation
- ○ simultaneous interaction[4]

All of these articulations speak to the type of collaborative and cooperative learning the LEOs are designed to support. The LEOs are not designed to be competitive or reward driven, but they are designed to address the complex and often competing needs of a diverse student population. Because the LEOs allow myriad ways in to learning, they can assist in developing student expertise and create equitable contributions from group members over time.

The ideas in this book are flexible enough to support a wide range of collaborative learning while also functioning as a more goal-focused, cooperative learning structure. This continuum is something for you to explore with your team over time.

About This Book

In the following chapters we articulate a flexible, differentiated, and collaborative approach to help secondary teachers and students purposefully engage with any text they might encounter in their world, from traditional print texts to nonprint texts like film and paintings, as well as the many hybrid texts found on the Internet, or environmental texts like rooms, houses, landscapes, or cities.

Chapter 1 articulates how you can use Learning Experience Organizers (LEOs) to make your curriculum pop. It introduces a ten-step process, describes the educational paradigm shifts involved, and discusses, in brief, the theory and research behind LEOs.

Chapter 2 walks you through a ten-step process to using LEOs in the classroom, while pointing out basic modifications. A model learning experience is outlined in each step, based on the film *Kit Kittredge*, along with example assessment rubrics.

Chapter 3 offers ideas for how to make LEOs a part of your unique classroom culture. It covers additional possibilities for designing learning experiences, shows detailed modifications—including ones for elementary

---

4. Kagan & Kagan, 2009.

classrooms and for students struggling with academic literacies, and presents some model LEOs.

Chapter 4 offers a wealth of resources, many of them involving less traditional text types than books and film. It guides you in locating information about the resources, helps you choose accompanying LEOs, and provides you with suggestions for using Twitter and other social networks to keep current on each text type.

Chapter 5 contains the fifty-five Learning Experience Organizers (LEOs), which are designed to help students make their thinking visible. Five student example LEOs are included at the beginning of the chapter to give you an idea of the variety of ways students might represent their thinking. All of the LEOs exist in digital form as customizable PDFs for you to share with your students. See page viii for the website link to download these forms.

The **Appendix**, available in the digital content, includes an extensive chart indicating the standards reflected in each LEO, including Common Core State Standards for English Language Arts and Math, as well as national science, social studies, and art standards.

You'll also find key terms defined and a list of resources by chapter to help ensure your understanding and guide you to further reading.

How to Use This Book

We hope our book is a catalyst for educators to bridge the divide between traditional and nontraditional texts and literacies to develop students' abilities to learn and think in teams. We also hope *Making Curriculum Pop* is an educative experience that allows teachers and students to develop literacies while exploring a wide range of texts.

Of course, this book was developed with feedback from our students, as well as preservice teachers and graduate students in our college classes. Its evolution is an ongoing process that we invite you to participate in. Please continue the conversation by sharing your experiences, thoughts, and ideas with us in our "MC POP—Developing Literacies in All Content Areas" group at the Making Curriculum Pop social network (mcpopmb.ning.com/group /mcpopdlaca).

If you are short on time, you can focus on Chapter 2 (the how-to chapter) and Chapter 5 (the LEO collection). Chapter 1 gives you the "why" of our LEOs. This chapter is excellent to get you into the mindset to make your curriculum pop while providing the research foundation supporting the practice. Chapter 4 is a dynamic place to spend time if you are looking to learn more about fresh, nontraditional texts for your classroom. This chapter might also be the most fun to dive into during a long weekend with a computer at your side.

In summary, we hope that the ideas and practices articulated in this book represent a small but meaningful contribution to make our schools and world a bit more engaging and humane while developing the type of cooperative practices that can inform a sustainable future for our planet. We hope the pedagogy outlined here helps all of us be more critical in our thinking, mindful in our metacognition, and kind to our students and colleagues as we learn and address challenges through inquiry and collaboration.

We'd love to hear how this book has helped you make your curriculum pop! If you have stories or questions for us, you can reach us through our publisher at help4kids@freespirit.com or through our social network at mcpopmb.ning.com.

Pam Goble and Ryan Goble

The **Making Curriculum Pop Ning** (also known as MC POP—mcpopmb.ning.com) is an online community for educators interested in better practices and more emotionally engaged classrooms through the exploration of popular and common cultures. MC POP is a free social network, but it is password protected; this allows educational materials to be shared under fair use practices. You can sign in using a Yahoo, Google, or Facebook ID. Once you join you can share and receive ideas from thousands of interesting educators from all over the world. We are also collecting your LEO ideas in the "MC POP—Developing Literacies in All Content Areas" group at the site with the idea that we will be able to share the best LEOs online.

CHAPTER 1

HOW CAN LEARNING EXPERIENCE ORGANIZERS (LEOs) MAKE YOUR CURRICULUM POP?

Using Learning Experience Organizers, or LEOs, creates a highly differentiated instructional practice designed to engage students with any print or nonprint text, including objects and spaces. Instead of using a traditional study guide to search for a text's "right answers," students can use LEOs to individually and then collaboratively interact with the text using a variety of specific and open-ended foci.

No idea comes out of thin air, and this book is no exception. Both of us have enhanced our language arts teaching using literature circles, a term and practice developed by Harvey Daniels in his watershed 1993 book *Literature Circles*. Daniels's unique practice popularized the idea that there can be individualized roles for exploration of differentiated literature. As we thought about his practice, we built on that work in three specific ways. We want to focus on:

1. incorporating print *and* nonprint texts

2. working across all content areas

3. utilizing roles that allow for whole-class, small-group, or individualized explorations of texts

What Daniels developed as literature circles and the role sheets that evolved, for us morphed into Learning Experience Organizers (LEOs) for students, as they read a wide range of texts independently and in different-sized groups across the curriculum.

Here, we think it is worth giving you a preview of a framework you can use to make your curriculum pop using the LEOs collected in Chapter 5. Chapter 2 takes you through a step-by-step progression for how students may explore texts, content, or themes using a selection of our fifty-five LEOs. No matter what texts you select or what LEOs you use, you will likely follow some permutation of the steps in Figure 1.1.

The concept of using LEOs for higher-level critical and creative thinking about any text evolved naturally through our work and research with a wide range of texts as we were working across the disciplines. We had developed specific LEOs for music, images, and film, but as the challenges teachers faced with nonprint texts became clearer, we set out to develop LEOs that went beyond media to include more nonprint texts like objects and spaces.

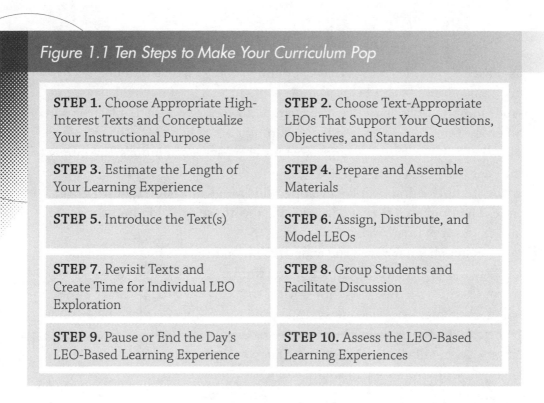

Figure 1.1 Ten Steps to Make Your Curriculum Pop

STEP 1. Choose Appropriate High-Interest Texts and Conceptualize Your Instructional Purpose

STEP 2. Choose Text-Appropriate LEOs That Support Your Questions, Objectives, and Standards

STEP 3. Estimate the Length of Your Learning Experience

STEP 4. Prepare and Assemble Materials

STEP 5. Introduce the Text(s)

STEP 6. Assign, Distribute, and Model LEOs

STEP 7. Revisit Texts and Create Time for Individual LEO Exploration

STEP 8. Group Students and Facilitate Discussion

STEP 9. Pause or End the Day's LEO-Based Learning Experience

STEP 10. Assess the LEO-Based Learning Experiences

Each of the fifty-five LEOs provided in Chapter 5 allow students to articulate unique insights and to work with other students to uncover (and as such, socially construct) the meaning and ideas presented in a text. The criteria, questions, and prompts central to our LEOs direct students to view any text more critically and creatively than they would using a standard worksheet. As a rule, most of the lower-level information (the basic information common to the bottom rungs of Bloom's Taxonomy—remembering, applying, and understanding) is easily uncovered while students—in groups and individually—craft unique, higher-level (analyzing, evaluating, and creating) connections, questions, and interpretations about the text using the LEOs.

It is also worth noting that Ron Ritchhart, Mark Church, and Karin Morrison stated in their book *Making Thinking Visible* that Bloom's Taxonomy remains a theory. They cite the work of Martha Stone Wiske at Harvard's Project Zero, whose team concluded that understanding is not a springboard to the higher levels of Bloom's Taxonomy but instead is a result of a mixture of application, analysis, evaluating, and creating. Ritchhart and his coauthors also remind us that "looking carefully to notice and fully describe what one sees can be an extremely complex and engaging task. Such close observation is at the heart of both science and art."[5]

Making Thinking Visible properly problematizes Bloom's Taxonomy while considering its usefulness. The collaborative and cooperative learning that

5. Ritchhart, et al., 2011, p. 6. •

our LEOs are designed for enables students to explore Bloom's Taxonomy as if each type of learning is a way of doing/being instead of a taxonomy one must climb. Each LEO is a single element in a larger flexible learning environment. Just as rivers, trees, birds, flowers, and insects play roles in an ecosystem, here every student—through his or her LEO—has a role to play. The LEOs are diverse and allow for every level of Bloom's Taxonomy to interact with each other toward deeper understandings. Students are given spaces to notice and deeply develop a wide range of understandings over time. The English Language Arts CCSS label these age-old practices as close and critical reading of complex texts.

Teachers have enjoyed the wide and varied range of foci we provide, and the way the LEOs direct their students' thinking. Our goal in using LEOs is to guide and structure students' critical thinking toward states of "flow"[6] in which the experience becomes natural and fun. While flow can be a scarce emotional state in schools built on the factory model of forty-five-minute classes, we regularly see LEOs create deep engagement around curriculum that pops for students and adults.

Engagement does not happen without frameworks. We offer LEOs as guidelines, structures, and models to help students and teachers interact more deeply with texts. We have purposely created LEOs individually and as a whole as flexible structures for students and teachers to customize as needed. It is also important to remember that LEOs are designed to guide students and teachers away from learning focused on the "right answer" and toward a collaborative classroom culture focused on "better answers." This design creates space for the unique voice of every student to be heard. To further that point, you'll see that we include a Wild Card LEO that allows a student to create a personalized lens to view a text.

LEOs can be seen as training wheels that can be removed over time or as something you continually mix up and explore. If the LEOs are used mindfully, they can be productive scaffolding for deeper learning. Differentiating the student LEOs, groupings, procedures, and texts, and encouraging collaborative discussions with the LEOs keeps them fresh and exciting over time.

We created LEOs to make learning more fun, but we also work in classroom and administrative roles and recognize how LEOs can hold students accountable. That said, we prefer to conceptualize LEOs as essential artifacts and powerful qualitative data that show footprints of student learning. In this role they can alleviate the fears of supervisors and parents who may question teachers using nonprint, "fluffy" texts in the classroom. Teachers can use the LEOs to share student work with colleagues, parents, and administrators and to showcase the fact that robust classroom practices are applied to nontraditional texts.

---

6. Csikszentmihalyi, 1997.

LEOs and Shifting Educational Paradigms

As stated in our introduction, we are interested in the double meanings of making curriculum pop. Obviously, our classes don't pop at every moment, or even on every day, but the goal of our work has been to approach every learning experience with an enthusiastic and collaborative spirit. We all know that challenging content like stoichiometry or Shakespeare can be taught in a flat, joyless way, or it can be an animated learning experience in which students collaborate around texts to make meaning, ponder, and perform in a vibrant learning community.

When we approach our classes, we are the lead learner. We don't think about this role as a performance, but we do think more like a member of a band or the producer of a Broadway show—we are trying to design a collaborative production for all kinds of people to share. We realize that every detail—from text selection to the choice of LEOs to the tone of our voice—can transform a class into an experience.

To shift away from the teaching mindset toward a learning experience mindset, we find it helpful to think about the legendary guitarist Jimi Hendrix. Hendrix could have named his group the Jimi Hendrix Band, Jimi Hendrix and the Little Wings, or simply used his name like many solo artists do. He chose to call the group the Jimi Hendrix *Experience* because that emphasized a major goal of his music.

Anyone who has seen the now-iconic film footage of Hendrix playing his guitar with his teeth, or behind his back, or burning and smashing his guitar at the climax of a song knows that this young artist was keenly aware of music's possibility to thrill an audience beyond the notes being played: it was not just music, but a tone, a stance, a way of dressing and being—in short, an experience.

Just as Hendrix's performance shifted the mindset and expectations of his audience, we hope you use the practices outlined in this book to shift your mindset and your students' expectations.

As Hendrix illustrated, the process of changing mindsets—and ultimately actions—can begin with words. As such, all five of our paradigm shifts begin with us renaming, redefining, and/or clarifying words, phrases, and mental models of teaching and learning.

Shift #1—From Reading Words of Text to Reading Worlds of Text

The introduction addressed our first semantic shift—*text* as an all-inclusive term. This definition has been present in theoretical literature for over half a century. As a result, teachers now view text in a far more comprehensive light to include more than just textbooks or novels.

When we are "reading" Jimi Hendrix's performance—the music, the outfit, his stance toward the audience, the lyrics, and his dramatic burning of the guitar—we are reading the word *and* the world.

Paulo Freire and Donaldo Macedo, in *Literacy: Reading the Word and the World*, explain why the world and the word begin to blur:

> Reading the world always precedes reading the word, and reading the word implies continually reading the world. As suggested earlier, this movement from the word to the world is always present; even the spoken word flows from our reading of the world. In a way, however, we can go further and say that reading the word is not preceded merely by reading the world, but by a certain form of *writing* it or *rewriting* it, that is, of transforming it by means of a conscious, practical work. For me, this dynamic movement is central to the literacy process.[7]

For this reason, the dynamic movement from word to world opens up a world of texts. However, because the field of literacy is still very much in flux, the idea of text has also been problematized. John Broughton, reflecting on the role of popular and visual culture in education, takes issue with the concept of text, for "the supremacy of literature over media, of textual over visual, appears absolute, the gap between high and low [culture, becomes] simply unbridgeable. . . . The appeal to text, then, and the aversion to image, to film or to visual culture in general, tend to link arms with parallel forms of social domination."[8]

We share Broughton's concerns while also recognizing that the word *text* is now a common term in K–12 teaching and policy documents and is central to the Common Core State Standards across the disciplines (although the expanded definition may not always be implied). For that reason we use the word *text* in the book so teachers enter into a world of body art, baseball cards, comics, cathedrals, pie charts, and power ballads. We hope educators conceptualize the word *text* as including all print and nonprint carriers of information as it relates to all the senses.

---

7. Freire & Macedo, 1987, p. 35.
8. Broughton, 2008, p. 29–30.

Shift #2—From Literacy to Literacies

The expansion of the concept of text runs parallel with expanded conceptions of literacy that began, most notably, with the New London Group's landmark treatise on multiliteracies. This has led to a shift in which educators are urged to conceptualize literacy not only as reading and writing but also to embrace what we like to call the "neglected literacies" of *speaking, listening, viewing,* and *representing*. To this list, we'd like to add *culling* (information in any form) and *collaborating,* as they have become points of emphasis in the information age and are centerpieces of every 21st century skills list (including the Common Core State Standards) that we have encountered.

Together, reading, writing, speaking, listening, viewing, representing, culling, and collaborating are essential literacies for those looking to critique or create in any medium/text. For that reason classrooms that "read the world" are more likely to engage learners and prepare them for success beyond their formal education.

Shift #3—From Teaching the Whats and Hows to Teaching the Whys

We strongly feel that every teacher has the opportunity to be a great leader. One of the most popular TED Talks is "How Great Leaders Inspire Action" by former ad man Simon Sinek, who turned the speech into a book titled *Start with Why*. In his book Sinek reminds us that, "Average companies [and organizations] give their people something to work on. In contrast, the most innovative organizations give their people something to work toward."[9] This idea and the research behind using clear "why" and purpose to animate our lives are clearly summarized in Daniel Pink's book *Drive*. We've all probably taught or participated in classes built on amassing rote skills and knowledge devoid of context, purpose, or "why." To this point, Pink cuts to the chase:

> It is often difficult to do something exceptionally well if we don't know the reason we're doing it in the first place. People at work [and school] are thirsting for context, yearning to know how what they do contributes to a larger whole. And a powerful way to provide that context is to spend a little less time telling how and a little more time showing why.[10]

What we're saying here is nothing new. From John Dewey to the standards movement to Wiggins and McTighe's *Understanding by Design*, people

9. Sinek, 2009, p. 96.
10. Pink, 2009, p. 138.

have been urging the articulation of a "why" or at least large points of inquiry to frame the all-too-pervasive "whats" and "hows." We wrote this book because we believe learning should be enthusiastic, meaningful, challenging, cooperative, and collaborative. That is the "why" behind this work. The Learning Experience Organizers (LEOs) in Chapter 5 are the "how" and the "what" to be determined by you and your students.

You might embrace our simple "why" of making curriculum pop, but LEOs are also waiting for your personalized "why." For each lesson we urge you to think carefully about why you want students to engage with a text, and we encourage you to make those reasons clear to your students. Great learning experiences should not be about compliance but about curiosity and engagement. Taking a little extra time to think about and articulate why we teach any given text or topic can make a world of difference.

One of the foci for preparing a better learning experience is to use Carol Ann Tomlinson's design for differentiation. Her articulation includes why students need to know something for real life. Articulating this purpose for or with students can give lessons powerful meaning and focus. It is important to remember that sometimes our "why" is revealed to us gradually over time, and this is an area our present school systems are not designed for. The purpose of any given lesson may end up differing from student to student and change over the course of a month, semester, year, or lifetime. In the Appendix in the digital content, we have aligned LEOs to a wide range of standards to help you align your learning experience after the fact. No matter how you use the LEOs, be sure to create spaces for sharing or uncovering this why/purpose during any given learning experience.

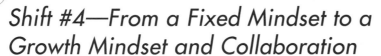

Shift #4—From a Fixed Mindset to a Growth Mindset and Collaboration

Another shift, much talked about in education but not easy to actualize, is based on Carol Dweck's groundbreaking research in the book *Mindset*. People with fixed mindsets about the ability to learn view every learning moment as a measure of innate worth and value—everything is a test of one's ability to perform in that moment. Most summative assessments are designed to look at just that.

On the flipside, those with growth mindsets see all learning as a way to expand a repertoire of skills and understanding, not as a simple win-or-lose proposition. This is what formative assessments are usually designed to assess. We have found this formative/growth mindset to be incredibly useful in our daily teaching with LEOs.

Our LEOs are open-ended, sometimes idiosyncratic, and—when selected well—easily accessible to a wide range of learners. Teachers quickly learn there are multiple ways of seeing a text and that purpose-driven collaboration and/or cooperation is better for learning and understanding. Students learn from each other, and when you split from shared LEO groups to mixed LEO groups, students learn more about their LEO before contributing to a larger group. While the majority of your LEO work making curriculum pop will be formative, there are situations where you might find ways to use LEO-based group learning experiences as summative assessments.

Here, collaboration makes everyone smarter. Obviously, there are many times when individual assessment is necessary and even preferred, but throughout most of our lives we grow and learn together. For this reason, LEOs should never be used in any type of competitive way, but instead should be used to cultivate ecosystems of shared learning.

We also think that teachers should approach this practice with a growth mindset. We hope that every time you experiment and play with LEOs, you will learn something new about your practice, yourself, your students, the texts you have selected, and—in your most sublime teaching moments— the world!

Shift #5—From Lesson to Learning Experience

The last, and perhaps most important, paradigm shift is about the type of instruction you're trying to create using LEOs. We don't want you to think about doing a LEO "lesson." We would rather you visualize the creation of a significant learning experience.

Making the shift from "planning a lesson" to "designing a learning experience" requires another semantic shift. The tools collected in Chapter 5 might typically be called "worksheets," "study guides," "role sheets," or even "graphic organizers," but we suggest the term Learning Experience Organizer—something we hope can become part of the lexicon of teaching and learning to help shift our thinking about the design of our instruction.

Though research supports the use of some type of guidance to understand materials being studied, an effective study guide should engage and elevate learning. Andrea Maxworthy cites two types of study guides: the interlocking and the noninterlocking (see Figure 1.2). The interlocking study guide is straightforward: it follows the text with answers that match exactly what is in the text. In other words, the interlocking study guide looks at what is present in the text.

The noninterlocking study guide looks at the relationship between the student and the text. Choice is a feature of this type of study guide, as is the opportunity to explore connections and feelings, make predictions, and focus on better responses (as opposed to those that are right or wrong). Noninterlocking study guides—such as our LEOs—incorporate higher-level thinking.

Figure 1.2 Interlocking vs. Noninterlocking Study Guides

Interlocking Traditional Study Guides/ Worksheets	Noninterlocking Learning Experience Organizers (LEOs)
○ Sometimes look for only the right answer	○ Look for a variety of responses
○ Usually are customized for one text	○ Created for multiple texts
○ Usually require an answer key	○ Generate student-centered responses or reflections
○ Designed with specific answers in mind	○ Develop frameworks for thinking and discussion and space for understanding
○ Focus on one modality	○ Value multiple ways of thinking
○ Accommodate one kind of learner	○ Allow for differentiation for many different types of learners
○ Designed to cover content	○ Designed to uncover content and allow for inference
○ Encourage little or no communication or collaboration among students	○ Encourage collaboration and communication

We like to couple these five paradigm shifts with the major research findings of a metastudy captured in the book *Powerful Learning*. There, Barron and Darling-Hammond showed that:

○ Students learn more deeply when they can apply classroom-gathered knowledge to real-world problems, and when they take part in projects that require sustained engagement and collaboration.

○ Active-learning practices have a more significant impact on student performance than any other variable, including student background and prior achievement.

○ Students are most successful when they are taught how to learn as well as what to learn.

These things are generally not happening when you simply deliver a lesson, ask students to take roles, or have students fill out worksheets, study guides, or graphic organizers. The findings of Darling-Hammond and Barron create a clear set of goals around active, student-centered, and collaborative learning with value far beyond studying for a chapter test.

Using LEOs to make your curriculum pop is directly aligned to Darling-Hammond and Barron's research, with one point of divergence: LEOs are not a traditional authentic assessment where we make students go outside the classroom to solve real-world problems. We do, however, believe that using popular and common texts brings issues that are authentic to the students' world into the classroom. Both these practices (bringing issues in and going beyond the classroom) can create spaces for more culturally responsive classrooms in which texts indigenous to the students' worlds are valued.

David Kirkland begins his brilliant book about the literacy of young black men, *A Search Past Silence*, by reminding readers:

> To be conceptually astute, I have not viewed literacy as natural, but as a consequence of those natural human drives that we may rightly call *the basics*—pleasure [flow], play, curiosity, creativity, and so on. Pleasure, play, curiosity, and creativity are prerequisite to one's love of learning (to read and write). As these basics invent themselves within the universe (within individuals and within the larger company of our inherited communities), the interdependent capacities/potentialities of languages and literacies, thought, and imagination are fully realized.[11]

LEOs are built on the energy of this passage, the pleasure of a great meal with family and friends, the freedom of a Jimi Hendrix solo, the curiosity of a Jane Goodall, and the creativity of you and your students. We (and likely Dr. Kirkland) know these are lofty aspirations. On paper, these paradigm shifts and research findings seem both reasonable and realistic. In practice, none of these shifts are easy. If that were the case, more schools would look radically different than they do today. Huge distances exist between knowing, understanding, and doing. We believe well-designed learning experiences are a powerful way to help teachers take the journey to a way of doing school that is considerably different than the status quo.

Recapping, we can shift our practice by . . .

○ **Reading Worlds of Text**—we can view the world as a place filled with texts, and value texts and issues authentic to the students' worlds.

○ **Shifting from Literacy to Literacies** by emphasizing a broad definition of the term *literacy* that includes reading, writing, listening, speaking, viewing, representing, culling (information), and collaborating.

○ **Teaching with Purpose** by thinking about the purpose or "why" of our lessons.

○ **Using a Growth Mindset**, i.e., LEOs are about learning, not performance.

○ **Cultivating Learning Experiences** by using collaborative and cooperative learning to create joyful learning ecosystems and significant learning experiences.

---

11. Kirkland, 2013, p. 8.

All these shifts are made in service of differentiated and flexible structures that shift student participation and idea generation to the forefront of instruction. With this mindset, we can start to visualize making curriculum pop with LEOs as an active, engaging, and meaningful practice that creates dynamic classrooms filled with fun and learning.

Theory and Research Behind Making Curriculum Pop with LEOs

Six interrelated strands of educational research and theory are integrated into the LEOs practice. Here are some brief (and simplified) summaries of the guiding ideas we use to make our curriculum pop.

Constructivism

LEOs are designed to move teachers to the sideline, allowing students to take the field to construct or uncover the meanings and content of a text.

Broadly speaking, constructivism is a theory that posits that knowledge is formed by the learners' own ideas and lived experiences. Constructivist teaching practices usually value collaboration, inquiry, active learning, social constructions of learning, and the unique ideas of each student. More specifically, constructivist teachers want students to generate their own creative ideas, questions, hypotheses, and interpretations. A constructivist teacher designs collaborative social learning experiences for students. Often this process has a clear purpose (a "why") and is problem- or inquiry-based.

Research shows that active learning can lead to better retention, comprehension, and possibilities for transference of knowledge across subjects and domains.[12] Ideas learned in one domain of school, play, work, or home can be fluidly applied in another setting and vice versa. LEOs are a powerful tool for learners to create meaningful relationships that link texts to the wider world.

Collaborative and Cooperative Learning

LEOs are designed to use the continuum of collaborative and cooperative learning that values individual insights and builds on them through a wide mix of collaborative structures and practices.

Even before they became buzzwords, collaborative and cooperative learning were recognized as valuable instructional practices. Those learning experiences are even more important today. In school, at home, and in work settings, it is clear that students need to be able to work creatively with

12. Bizar & Daniels, 1998; Darling-Hammond et al., 2008; Hattie, 2011; Marzano, Pickering, & Pollack, 2001; Perkins & Salomon, 1994.

diverse groups of people. While the myth of the singular genius persists, many creativity researchers are keenly attuned to the role colleagues and collaborators play in every breakthrough, big and small.[13]

Students who have meaningful collaborative learning experiences develop critical and creative thinking skills. Cooperative learning is also one of the nine effective strategies cited in Marzano, Pickering, and Pollack's landmark book *Classroom Instruction That Works*. Robert Slavin suggests two examples of cooperative learning that work well with the LEOs: (1) jigsaws and (2) four-member groups which are diverse.[14] Both collaborative and cooperative learning encourage peer communication and foster social behaviors in a group setting. These skills are key objectives in the Common Core State Standards.

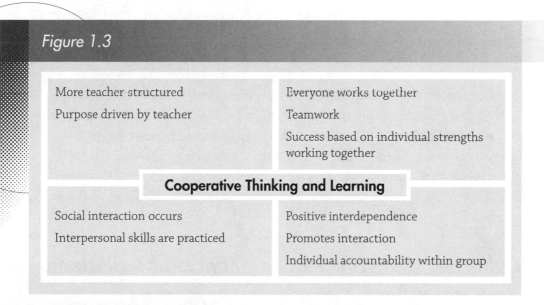

Figure 1.3

More teacher-structured	Everyone works together
Purpose driven by teacher	Teamwork
	Success based on individual strengths working together

Cooperative Thinking and Learning

Social interaction occurs	Positive interdependence
Interpersonal skills are practiced	Promotes interaction
	Individual accountability within group

Figure 1.4

Students search for understanding through problem solving	Groups work together, valuing individual voices but focusing on the group product
More student-driven	
Student talk	

Collaborative Thinking and Learning

Social interaction occurs	Deepen thinking
Interpersonal skills are valued	Expressive
	New knowledge generated by group

---

13. Csikszentmihalyi, 1997; Gardner, 1994; John-Steiner, 2000.
14. Slavin, 1991.

Cultural Studies and Media Education

LEOs value deep readings and critical evaluations of popular and common cultures in classrooms.

Cultural studies is a deeply interdisciplinary field that borrows from many branches of social sciences, humanities, and the arts. Cultural studies scholars believe that popular and common cultures—known in these circles as "symbol systems"—can yield a wide range of scientific, historical, political, cultural, and anthropological insights to the mindful learner. One of Ryan's favorite essays in this field is from John Fiske's anthology *Reading the Popular,* where he "reads all the signs and symbols on the beach" in his native Australia.

Whereas cultural studies emphasizes things like politics, power, race, gender, and pleasure, media education and media literacy in the United States tend to focus a bit more directly on how students access, evaluate, produce, and critically analyze nonprint texts (as opposed to their surrounding issues) and are more closely tied to art appreciation and literacy movements. Both fields are used across a wide range of content areas.

LEOs are inspired by work in both of these fields, without being a pure outgrowth of either. A LEO such as the Framer (what is seen and not seen) is an example of a lens influenced by both fields. Depending on the LEOs you choose, you can "do" digital and media literacy, media education, or cultural studies in your discipline based on your understandings of these practices.

Culturally Relevant Teaching/Engaging Students in Learning

LEOs allow for crosscultural and multicultural understandings by creating opportunities for personal beliefs, values, and cultures to be affirmed and explored through texts.

Referring back to Kirkland, we believe that "pleasure, play, curiosity, and creativity are prerequisite to one's love of learning." Students enjoy LEOs, and from what we have experienced, the open-ended nature of the LEOs create learning spaces that encourage deeper exploration of texts. We think this happens because the LEOs are designed to value many perceptions, backgrounds, and points of view. Students are far more detailed and intense about their practice of reading text when they use LEOs. LEOs encourage culturally responsive teaching environments that value texts created by the diverse cultural and social groups students might identify with. This type of teaching also encourages popular cultures to be brought into the classroom as a pathway to engagement. Expanding our ideas about literacy more often than not creates engaging classroom cultures where deep reading, critical thinking, and creative interpretations are collaboratively developed with peers.

With the explosion of established technologies like Facebook and Twitter and with the development of newer platforms like Snapchat and Whatsapp (dating our work as we write these), nonprint and digital texts will only continue to become more prevalent facets of youth culture.

At the same time challenges like climate change will require us to read our neighborhoods, cities, and common spaces more carefully as well. Relevant, culturally connected teaching and learning should embrace the use of nonprint texts as a powerful practice that engages learners in meaning-making across the disciplines.

Engagement with a text and community of learners is an antecedent to learning. When you value students' cultures, points-of-view, and ways of seeing and doing, texts become culturally relevant. For that reason we have put a premium on developing a practice that engages students that is the heart of Lev Vygotsky's zone of proximal development, where the tasks and texts you ask students to do should be in the "Goldilocks zone" where students are challenged but not overwhelmed and unable to enter into a learning experience.

By making space for culturally relevant texts and open-ended ways to respond to them, we increase the probability that students will be able to participate in a learning experience. An emphasis on texts that are authentic to students' worlds, that are created by diverse creators, and that make students curious about their worlds creates learning ecosystems where everyone's skills and voices have value.

Differentiation of Instruction and Multiple Intelligences

LEOs are designed to give students and teachers myriad ways into texts, differentiating content, process, and product based on learners' readiness, interests, and learning profile.

For the last twenty years education circles have been buzzing about differentiated instruction (DI) in classrooms. We find that many teachers are confused about the parameters or definition of differentiation. Furthermore, DI is often spoken of as a new practice, but differentiation has been embedded in education since the fluid grade levels and individualized teaching of the one-room schoolhouse. *Differentiation* refers to a teaching practice designed to support diverse groups of learners with different learning styles, strengths, and weaknesses as they search for unique pathways to learning.

Differentiation authority Carol Ann Tomlinson believes that the practice "is like jazz. It is constant improvisation, based on solid themes and shared experiences."[15] Silver, Strong, and Perini take the concept of differentiation further and carefully consider a student's learning type, i.e., specific learning that emphasizes mastery, understanding, self-expression, and interpersonal skills.

Differentiated practices allow teachers to reflect on their teaching in order to make sure they find ways to connect with students' learning styles. We have created a wide range of LEOs so that students can explore a wide range of content. While "better answers" should emerge over time as students collaborate with LEOs, the LEOs have no answer keys. Every student's unique observations and interpretations create unique individual and group footprints of learning. LEOs can be used in a multitude of ways to support a wide range of differentiated practices and make those connections, as we explain in Chapters 3 and 4. There are many ways in because the LEOs are informed by multiple intelligences.

> While "better answers" should emerge over time as students collaborate with LEOs, the LEOs have no answer keys. Every student's unique observations and interpretations create unique individual and group footprints of learning.

The concept of multiple intelligences offers ways to see the world through many different lenses. Howard Gardner describes nine types of intelligence (with the possibility of more in the future) to convey different ways of learning: verbal/linguistic, mathematical/logical, visual, kinesthetic, naturalistic, musical, interpersonal, intrapersonal, and existential. All of the intelligences are represented in our LEOs. Gardner's and Thomas Armstrong's research on multiple intelligences asks teachers to focus not on "how smart students are" but on "how students are smart." For this reason, you'll find LEOs designed for students who excel at a wide range of skills. You can use them to support the intelligences in which students excel as well as the ones that they struggle with. Either way, it is a win-win opportunity for learning, critical thinking, and social as well as intellectual growth.

For example, for kinesthetic students we have the Performer LEO that asks them to create a performance or physical tableau of the texts they read, and we also have LEOs like the Body Linguist and Casting Director that allow students to focus on physical traits. In many cases those students will use their faces and bodies to communicate physical acts and expressions in small-group discussions. Multiple LEOs (e.g., Cartoonist, Framer, Mapper, and Visualizer) allow for visual students to draw. Soundtrack Supervisor and Sound Mixer are designed to support musical intelligences. Naturalists are asked to focus on the climate and the ecosystem captured by a text. Of course, not every LEO will work for every text, but there is a wide range of possibilities for every learning experience.

---

15. Tomlinson, 2003, p. xiii.

Literacy Across the Curriculum and New Literacies

LEOs address the need for teachers and students in every discipline to help students develop their ability to read, write, listen, speak, view, and represent.

In *Active Literacy Across the Curriculum*, Heidi Hayes-Jacobs reminds her readers that:

> [W]hether it is listening to directions, reading a passage, writing a response, or discussing a point of view, the individual student's ability to perform and grow in a classroom rests squarely on his or her corresponding language capacity. The reading, writing, speaking and listening strategies necessary for student engagement cut across disciplines.[16]

Being literate today also encompasses the ability to critically and intelligently view and represent text. In many ways William Kist's characteristics of "New Literacies" classrooms are also a robust way of thinking about literacy in a wide range of very modern texts. The characteristics include the following:

- New Literacies classrooms feature daily work in multiple forms of representation.

- In such classrooms, there are explicit discussions of the merits of using certain symbol systems in certain situations (such as when conveying a concept, advertising a product, or expressing an emotion), and the students are given many choices about the kinds of texts they read and write.

- There are think-alouds by the teacher, who models working through problems using symbol systems such as video production, website design, and print writing.

- Students take part in a mix of individual and collaborative activities.

- New Literacies classrooms are places of student engagement in which students report achieving "flow" state.[17]

The various literacies—reading, writing, speaking, listening, viewing, and representing, as well as culling and collaborating—require attention in every discipline. These objectives are further reinforced by the Common Core State Standards.

16. Hayes-Jacobs, 2006, p. 3.
17. Kist, 2004.

While each LEO might not specifically address every discipline in any given context, they are designed as a universal strategy to develop literacies that can be applied to explore texts in multiple disciplines.

Creativity rules here, in that you can use LEOs in many domains depending on your purpose. For teachers outside language arts concerned with testing, it is important to realize that every test is a literacy test before it is a content test. For example, the science sections of most standardized tests consist almost entirely of reading passages coupled with graphs and images. Even if a student understands every concept in a passage about ways in which the circulatory system might become obstructed, he or she will still need to read deeply to tease out detail, argument, context clues, main ideas, and leaps of logic in order to answer questions.

21st Century Skills

LEOs are designed to replicate the types of skills essential for global citizens like communication, creativity, critical thinking, collaboration, and information literacy.

Here there is some overlap with collaborative learning and new literacies, but 21st century skills are more focused on human capital around the skills required for employment. The Partnership for 21st Century Learning described the essential skills that students will need to know and be able to do in the 21st century global village. This work echoes the work of Tony Wagner, who articulated global competencies in *The Global Achievement Gap*. These ideas were popularized in books like journalist Daniel H. Pink's *A Whole New Mind* and *Drive*.

These and other related frameworks share common concepts like decentralization, performance, role play, empathy, storytelling, collaboration, synthesis, pattern recognition, play, and interdisciplinary thinking. It is clear that we are in a historical moment where our virtual and actual worlds are filled with complex texts (think of understanding and mitigating global warming as an example) that—to be read with the most clarity—require collaboration and hard-to-measure skills, ideas, and "ways of doing" to illuminate our schools and our futures.

Taken as a whole, the aforementioned organizations and thinkers believe we must learn to read a wide range of interdisciplinary texts to achieve gainful employment, have economic success, address inequalities, and stabilize our deteriorating climate and ecosystems. At the individual level students and teachers must use the reading of texts as a way to find purpose, meaning, and enjoyment in their lives. As mentioned earlier, we have tried to distill these concepts into two additional literacies, "culling" and "collaborating," around a wide range of texts.

CHAPTER 2

HOW TO USE LEOs IN THE CLASSROOM

This chapter is designed to walk you through some ins and outs of using LEOs to make your curriculum pop. We will guide you through *one way* to do this while pointing out basic modifications. Chapter 3 will cover additional possibilities, detailed modifications (including ones for students struggling with academic literacies and for elementary classroom settings), and some model LEOs.

The more you use LEOs to create learning experiences, the more you will customize, remix, and reimagine ways to use these tools. We expect and encourage the creation of LEO variations that work for you and your students and urge you to share those LEO ideas at the Making Curriculum Pop Ning in the "MC POP—"Developing Literacies in All Content Areas" group (mcpopmb.ning.com/group/mcpopdlaca).

This book and the LEOs included in it are designed as differentiated learning tools to develop literacy across the curriculum in upper-elementary and secondary classrooms. We have also had great success using them without any modifications in our undergraduate and graduate classes. A majority of the LEOs in Chapter 5 can be used in every discipline. Because there are fifty-five LEOs, you have to select those that are the strongest matches with the texts you want to explore.

Making Curriculum Pop with LEOs

"Mixing things up" is the hallmark of any truly differentiated and student-centered practice—every text and context yields unique procedures and outcomes. With this in mind, LEOs are designed to be different for every teacher and learner in a variety of subjects, grade levels, and settings.

At their core LEOs create a differentiated collaborative learning experience where each student explores texts and develops literacies through different lenses. The whole class may explore one text, groups of students may be looking at individual texts, or students might be selecting texts around a theme or type of content. We always recommend that the student is first given time to explore and respond individually through a LEO and then in mixtures of small and large groups. The duration of your LEO experience will vary widely depending on your texts and objectives.

As you begin developing a LEO practice, we suggest using short film clips as a powerful starting point. Because film integrates many disciplines and modalities (sound, writing, set and costume design, photography, acting), it allows for the widest range of LEO choices.

As any designer will tell you, form follows function. Just as the LEOs collected here are differentiated in a way that allows multiple ways of being appropriate (form), there are multiple ways you can create a LEOs experience (function). As mentioned in previous sections, you can use the LEOs in more collaborative and student-guided ways or in more structured cooperative learning formats. If you or your students are familiar with literature circles, that format provides a strong mental model to build off of. If you are not familiar with literature circles, don't panic—keep calm and read on.

As we guide you through the more general steps for using LEOs, we share a specific example of a learning experience built around short film clips from the feature film *Kit Kittredge: An American Girl*. We have listed two clips on page 34—either one is excellent for a two-day learning experience.

Ten Steps to Designing Learning Experiences

Note: for a helpful visual, see Figure 1.1 on page 13 in Chapter 1.

Step   1. Choose Appropriate High-Interest Texts and Conceptualize Your Instructional Purpose.
Step   2. Choose Text-Appropriate LEOs That Support Your Questions, Objectives, and Standards.
Step   3. Estimate the Length of Your Learning Experience.
Step   4. Prepare and Assemble Materials.
Step   5. Introduce the Text(s).
Step   6. Assign, Distribute, and Model LEOs.
Step   7. Revisit Texts and Create Time for Individual LEO Exploration.
Step   8. Group Students and Facilitate Discussion.
Step   9. Pause or End the Day's LEO-Based Learning Experience.
Step 10. Assess the LEO-Based Learning Experience.

Step 1: Choose Appropriate High-Interest Texts and Conceptualize Your Instructional Purpose

We usually start with some very broad content, question, theme, or skill in our minds as we select texts. Our instructional purpose usually has a vague outline when we're thinking about texts to teach with. More often than not, we encounter a text that moves, surprises, or engages us in memorable ideas.

As we think alone and with colleagues, texts start to dictate questions, standards, objectives, and purposes as they relate to our class. Starting with a standard, question, or text becomes a very "chicken-and-egg" type discussion. It does not matter where you begin, but for best results your text should be linked to a big idea—a theme or essential question that is compelling and ripe for cognitive dissonance. That is to say, rich texts tend to have sufficient detail and context to allow for conflicting ideas, points of view, and interpretations.

During this process you might discover that a text helps you refine and revise your theme, essential questions and objectives, or learning targets.

> At their core LEOs create a differentiated collaborative learning experience where each student explores texts and develops literacies through different lenses.

In other situations choosing high-interest texts might be part of collaboration with your students to refine your questions, objectives, texts, and their connections to standards. No matter how you plan it, it is usually a give-and-take process; the processes and templates are designed to be flexible and organic.

You may want to start planning with a standard. This is certainly doable, but if you are not thinking about the big picture (the "why" of your text), your lesson might not pop with students. If you have a rich text and powerful question, the LEOs allow you to align to standards after the fact (see the Appendix in the digital content).

The most effective LEO-based learning experiences are usually built around texts that are **connected** (to students, multiple disciplines, standards, objectives, questions, and culture) and **relevant** to students' lives. This does not mean you have to choose hit songs, blockbuster movies, or up-to-the-minute websites. Sometimes familiarity is helpful to your objectives; sometimes it is not.

While artistic exemplars of any medium can be incredible texts for study (think Oscar-winning films, the Beatles, St. Paul's Cathedral, the paintings of Basquiat, or the gardens at the Palace of Versailles), you will also find less well-known or obscure (in the critical sense) texts that can be fruitful sources of discussion. Sometimes you can learn just as much exploring the design of a website like Facebook as you can by looking at a less successful website in the same genre, like Google+. Cultural studies advocates are quick to remind us that seemingly mundane architecture, schlocky science fiction films, gossip websites, popular clothing, and shopping malls can be rich sites of study if they align with your teaching objectives and LEOs.

Rich texts usually make people curious by being novel, complex, ambiguous, and variable, depending on your point of view. Rich texts in any medium provide myriad opportunities for diverse responses that move students toward deep understandings. These texts, coupled with LEOs, allow students to practice their critical, creative, and reflective thinking. As a (bendable) rule of thumb, you can generally assess the richness of a text by the number of LEOs that can be used to explore it; the more LEO options you have, the more likely you're using a rich and varied text.

When designing an interdisciplinary unit for William Golding's novel *Lord of the Flies* with a team of teachers, Ryan and the group came up with the question "Are humans animals?" While the biological answer is simple, the conceptual question is complex. This essential question allowed the teaching team to introduce texts that made connections between behaviors that are perceived as human and those that are perceived as animal. These texts include short documentaries about the Stanford Prison Experiment (where undergrads assumed the roles of jailers and inmates, treating each other so brutally that the study had to be shut down), news clips about high school hazing, bullying, the movie *Mean Girls* (you might remember the scene where cat sounds animate a cafeteria fight), the graphic novel *Maus* (animals are anthropomorphized as human), science documentary clips about animal intelligence and language, and articles about legal initiatives designed to give animals the same rights as humans.

These texts built on the animal behavior of characters in *Lord of the Flies* and forced students to consider the conceptual boundaries around concepts of humans and animals. Excerpts from these texts, some of which were explored using LEOs, helped animate the novel by enhancing and problematizing its themes and issues.

The aforementioned process used multiple possible texts in service of a single essential question; for the purposes of this chapter, we will take you through the process with one model using *Kit Kittredge*.

In the late 1980s, the American Girl Company began creating dolls linked to books featuring girls from different historical periods. By the beginning of the 21st century, American Girl dolls were a phenomenon—the books and dolls expanded into movies and a chain of high-end retail stores. We found this popular culture text to be a powerful teaching tool, especially through the film *Kit Kittredge: An American Girl*. This film is the type of popular or common text that appears simple, but when viewed with appropriate LEOs one quickly notices how loaded it is with content, concepts, and questions. Many students—including the boys—have some familiarity with the text because American Girl books and dolls have become a part of youth culture. *Kit Kittredge* is multilayered: it features multiple conflicts, novel technologies, economic indicators, outdated cultural practices, unique sounds, music, and slang. These elements allow for many levels of reading with a wide range of LEOs.

The clips we chose are of high interest to students because they explore big ideas like the Great Depression, hobo culture, homelessness, economic hardship, and themes around trust and friendship through the eyes of preteen protagonists. The selected clips can connect to multiple disciplines, with music, language arts, social studies, economics, health, math, and science being the obvious connections.

Lastly, the film is relatable to its intended audience of upper-elementary and middle school students, and though it uses familiar vocabulary, it also pushes students to learn new words and background knowledge. In cognitive science terms, the text falls within a student's zone of proximal development for most middle school students: not too hard to read nor too easy, yet challenging, which encourages students to persevere.

As a result of these traits, the film is a great "a-ha" text for students in grades six through twelve, as well as for student teachers and practicing teachers. Without fail the clips yield fascinating discussions about relatives who lived through the Depression and discussions about why people struggled with certain technologies that no longer exist today.

Either of the two clips described below is excellent to use for a model.

Clip I: 25:10–27:42 Kit Writes a Letter to Her Father Explaining How They Are Saving Money.
SET UP: Kit's dad must move from Cincinnati to Chicago to find work, leaving his family behind because of the Great Depression.

START: Kit's dad (actor Chris O'Donnell) boards a bus for Chicago.

FINISH: Kit: "Mother says, 'It's magic,' but the real magician is our newest arrival . . ."

Jefferson Berk: ". . . Jefferson J. Berk, master of misdirection, dean of deception, and escape artist extraordinaire."

Clip II: 37:06–41:57 Kit Tours a Hobo Camp So She Can Write a Newspaper Article.
You can cut at multiple spots for discussion or go to the end.

SET UP: On assignment for the local newspaper, Kit asks her hobo friends (who help out at her house) if she can visit the hobo camp/jungle.

START: Kit: "I was thinking about doing a story about you and Countee, Will, if you let me."

FINISH: Kit: "When times are tough, people like to blame someone, and hobos are an easy target, I guess."

While *Kit Kittredge: An American Girl* serves as a nice exemplar, many factors are at play when selecting texts. Here are some ideas we have developed that guide our process.

Figure 2.1 Ways of Teaching Popular and Common Cultures

Stand Alone/Independent Text

Most popular culture texts we select for teaching are rich enough to stand alone as curriculum in and of themselves; more complicated texts can merit two to four weeks of instruction.

Text as Direct Link to Core Curricula

Texts used as direct links make direct connections to core text or concept. They generally enhance and amplify student engagement and understanding.

Rorschach Text as Thematic Focal Point

Texts used as Rorschach are most effective to focus attention, amplify, reflect, and reinforce a curricular theme.

STAND ALONE/INDEPENDENT TEXT

Most popular culture texts we select for teaching are rich enough to **stand alone** as curriculum, in and of themselves. In fact, more complicated texts can merit two to four weeks of instruction. When looking at these common or popular texts, you can explore the content in conjunction with issues unique to a particular discipline. The practices of text education and cultural studies allow you to look at texts in terms of such things as production, audience, ideology, history, politics, dominance, subordination, power (hegemony), classicism, sexism, homophobia, racism, representation, values, positionality, power, and social implications. Because many texts exemplify Marshall McLuhan's famous saying, "the medium is the message," it is essential to emphasize the elements and techniques used by text producers to add meaning. Additionally, this acknowledges that pleasure and fun are essential elements to be embraced when teaching with popular and common texts.

DIRECT LINK: TEXT-TO-CORE-CURRICULA CONTENT

Texts used as **direct links** make direct connections to a core text or concept. They generally enhance and amplify student engagement and understanding. Any *Schoolhouse Rock* song would be an example of this, e.g., using the song "I'm Just a Bill" to explain how bills become laws. Teaching John Steinbeck's novel *The Grapes of Wrath* using Bruce Springsteen's album *The Ghost of Tom Joad,* using Andrew Niccol's film *Gattaca* to teach genetics, or teaching real-world applications of math by using infographics or blueprints are all examples of this method.

RORSCHACH: TEXT AS THEMATIC FOCAL POINT

Named after the famous psychological test developed in the 1960s, the text as **Rorschach** is most effective to focus attention, amplify, reflect, and reinforce a curricular theme. These texts lend themselves to multiple interpretations based on your personality, culture, point of view, or context.

These texts are often thematically linked to something you want to explore or study in class, but they lack the detail and specificity of the other two categories (stand alone and direct link). Many short films, clips, still images, advertisements, or songs can be used this way. Often these texts might have more of a postmodern/abstract bent or are simple musings on the human condition. A Beatles song like "Revolution" could be used to discuss the French Revolution or Archimedes's "Eureka" moment when he discovered how to calculate volume.

BIG GUIDING QUESTIONS FOR TEACHERS TO CONSIDER

1. What curricular content do you want to explore with this text?

2. What themes or main ideas of the text interest you?

3. Is this text appropriate for your students developmentally and culturally?

4. What teaching objectives and/or Common Core State Standards do you want to align with this text?

5. Is this text layered? Are there multiple levels of meaning and possibility for analysis?

6. What connections can you make between this text and other classes, disciplines, and student life experiences?

7. What approach (stand alone, direct link, or Rorschach) seems like the strongest starting point for your teaching of the text?

8. How many LEOs can be used with this text? The more LEOs you can apply, the more options you have for differentiated instruction.

Number three merits some brief elaboration. Obviously, you won't choose to screen a film with graphic sexuality or listen to a podcast loaded with inappropriate language, but it is essential that you *always preview texts in their entirety*. Don't put yourself in a position to be surprised by a text. As long as you make mindful choices around texts and use the LEOs as artifacts/data that demonstrate student learning, you will develop a successful learning experience. If you are unsure about a text for *any* reason, double-check with your supervising administrator and/or send home permission slips. You will probably be using sound instructional judgment, but unexpected concerns can always pop up in a community.

OTHER POINTS OF CONSIDERATION

1. Are there any special or interesting circumstances surrounding the production of, public response to, or uses of the text? Are there things students might want to know about the text's creator(s)?

2. What are the interesting or unique features/characteristics of the text? For example, if you are studying or producing a music text, you might look at timbre, tone, mood, melody, harmony, rhythm, dynamics, tempo, meter, instrumentation, editing, or sound effects that merit further analysis. If you are studying a biological ecosystem, you might look for biotic and abiotic components, closed or open systems, native or invasive species or the transformation of energy in the space. In this case your way of looking at a song or ecosystem is illustrative of a layered text.

3. What other texts connect with the texts you've selected? Don't be afraid to ask students to make connections here as well.

4. What text-specific terms or vocabulary may need to be understood to make meaning of the text?

5. What understandings (prior knowledge) or misunderstandings might students bring to the text, and how can you activate students' prior knowledge to make your lesson more meaningful? This question helps you select the most useful LEOs.

6. Does this text reflect on or comment on societal norms and values? If so, how?

Step 2: Choose Text-Appropriate LEOs That Support Your Questions, Objectives, and Standards

You want your text and LEOs to connect with the essential question, instructional objectives, or standards related to your unit. These larger frameworks for designing significant learning experiences give texts additional meaning and enhance student engagement. Asking yourself the classic "what do I want the students to know and be able to do?" question is a solid starting point with any text.

Moving beyond these goals, it is important to remember that every student brings different skills, talents, and learning styles to each task, which is one of many reasons it is important to differentiate instruction. Many people think they differentiate well if they do ability grouping. This is a form of differentiation, but a truly differentiated practice really mixes things up. Great differentiated learning experiences adjust content, process, and product around student readiness, interests, and learning styles on a regular basis. Our LEOs help teachers develop this type of multifaceted differentiated practice.

Adjusting LEOs for individual students (and texts) is part of developing a differentiated practice that makes your curriculum pop. LEOs allow students to explore new areas of knowledge and understanding, but they also help develop and showcase students' skills.

Most bodybuilders do not only work on getting large biceps—they do exercises designed to develop the entire body. You can imagine LEOs as different exercises and weight machines at a gym. Each one is designed to develop different skills and neurological pathways. For example, if a student is an artist, the opportunity to showcase his or her talents using the Visualizer LEO is a positive outcome. A student for whom artistic talent is not a strength but who chooses to try this LEO is challenged, and the new experience develops underutilized skills. Both of these are win-win situations. (When you get to step 6 and students are self-selecting LEOs, you can encourage them by saying something like, "I'd like you to choose a LEO that is a strength/challenge for you today.")

Traditional study guides generally look for single right answers and rely on the teacher (or answer key) to judge correct and incorrect answers. LEOs, on the other hand, allow for a wide range of answers. The best part about this for you, as the teacher, is that you will constantly learn new or interesting things from your students about texts because LEOs generate so many unique interpretations.

LEOs are designed to distribute the exploration of a text across an entire class; however, some may require more work than others. When looking at (and assessing) LEOs, keep in mind that fair is not always equal. Some students might enjoy the higher-level LEOs like Wonderer, while others may be more comfortable hunting for vocabulary words with the Wordsmith LEO. Interestingly, while the Wonderer LEO requires more complex thinking, the Wordsmith might require more work. The Wordsmith might have to review or listen to a text to make sure he or she heard all the vocabulary words, and then look up all the definitions at the computer. Does this mean a Wonderer did less and a Wordsmith did more work? Is this an unfair distribution of tasks? We believe this division of labor is a hallmark of differentiation, cooperative learning, and real-world collaboration.

You can narrow your choice of LEOs by reflecting on your teaching objectives. If you are using the *Kit Kittredge* clip in a language arts class, you might have objectives linked to characters' actions and choices (character development) or some of the dramatic elements of the text (conflict, plot, symbolism, etc.). This could lead to the use of LEOs such as the Dialogue Master, Plot Master, or Sociologist.

In a math or economics class, you might use this clip to explore the scarcity of resources or the variables affecting Americans' lives and incomes during the Great Depression. LEOs that might align here are the Economist, Fact Checker, Information Designer, Cryptographer, X-cavator, and the Data Analyst.

In a science class you might want to explore human health (see the hobo camp in clip two), migration, or the development of household technologies. For those purposes, LEOs like the Archaeologist, Blogger, Climate & Culture Analyst, Ecologist, or Predictor might do the trick.

The broad categories of LEOs allow students to look at texts through a wide range of lenses without overwhelming them. At the top of each LEO students are asked to fill in what type of text they are looking at. Each LEO has a space for the student's name and, if needed, the names of people in the group.

> As long as you make mindful choices around texts and use the LEOs as artifacts/data that demonstrate student learning, you will develop a successful learning experience.

Obviously, certain texts have overlapping types because they are multimodal; for example, a comic or graphic novel could be both visual and print. A webpage could be interpreted primarily as digital text, but it may also have visual, audio, and print elements. In these situations, students should feel free to list multiple categories, or they might decide to list its primary text mode. The categories are never absolutes.

We are careful to choose LEOs that will fit the text and that might yield the richest responses. If you're looking at a series of photographs, you probably won't choose the Soundtrack Supervisor or Sound Mixer LEOs because the images will not be loaded with audible sounds. You should start with the LEOs that get you curious, engaged, interested, or excited about exploring a text with your students, and as students get familiar with the LEOs they can choose those that excite them. If you don't know where to begin, LEOs that work with most texts that use language include Connector, Highlighter, Visualizer, Wonderer, and Wordsmith.

As you become more adventurous, you can consult the lists in Chapter 4 of suggested LEOs uniquely suited to texts in each medium. Even with these guidelines, we hope you will explore the whole palette of LEOs and even design your own (see Chapter 3 for more on this). Not all the LEOs will be used all of the time, but we work hard to offer our students more LEOs than they need so they have a choice, a point we will elaborate on in step 6.

For this model experience using the film *Kit Kittredge*, we choose a **content objective** that dovetails with social studies and/or language arts classes. Our working objective can be to develop students' background knowledge about the Great Depression and how it impacted the daily lives of Americans. We might also have a **skill objective** like "close reading of a text," but for this model we're going to focus on the content objective above.

Of course, one way to cover these objectives would be by assigning readings from any standard history textbook coupled with traditional study guide questions. Because this type of instruction often focuses on one or two learning styles or types of multiple intelligences and generates a single product, it is not likely to engage students actively or prompt them to ask questions or make individual connections with the text. High-interest texts paired with LEOs create a highly differentiated and collaborative learning experience that uncovers a wide range of content based on students' individual foci, process, and product related to our objectives.

Because the *Kit Kittredge* clips are laden with content, almost any LEO could be used. Given our objective to build students' background knowledge, we selected LEOs like Fashion Critic, Tech Specialist, Economist, and Wordsmith to meet that goal.

If you're concerned that students will not succeed initially with four LEOs, you can scale down the process by modeling two LEOs. If you make that choice, we recommend two that require the higher-level thinking: Economist and Tech Specialist. Both of these LEOs assist students with a skill that the Common Core State Standards refer to as deep or close reading.

The Economist LEO is interesting to use because these clips don't take place in an obvious setting like a grocery store where produce and products are clearly labeled with large price signs. Students need to infer things about the economics in the text. In the first clip, Kit explains in a letter to her father that they are using Aunt Millie's "Waste Not Want Not" recipe for bread, where they cut a single slice into four pieces to make it last longer. In another scene Kit narrates that her family is taking on boarders to bring in additional income. And in the second clip she explains that the newspaper will pay her "a penny a word for freelance." All of these details are clues about the economics of the time period.

In a similar vein the Tech Specialist LEO requires students to view the text with a wide-angle lens, looking for anything that might be considered technology. This is a unique way to view the film, as students have to scan for things like toasters, clotheslines, telephones, typewriters, and modes of transportation. Finding this diverse and (to us) outdated set of technologies requires a careful exploration of the text.

Step 3: Estimate the Length of Your Learning Experience

With LEOs (and our teaching in general) we try to do as much as possible with small chunks of text in order to maximize instructional time around individual and collaborative LEO work time. As a baseline we budget at least two class periods for LEO-based learning experiences with brief texts, in any medium that students can explore individually (view, listen, read, surf, or study), in ten to twenty-five minutes, with time added for reexploration of any text.

Two big benefits of using shorter texts are (1) they make it easier to budget time for reexploration, and (2) they often inspire students to complete the full text, or find related texts on their own, outside of school. Generally our goal is to explore the texts in class, to socially construct meaning with peers.

Although LEOs work with longer texts too, you will probably have more success breaking the text into chunks and assigning different LEOs to each student for each chunk. For example, if you choose to explore something like a sixty-minute *This American Life* radio show episode or a feature film, it is valuable to have students do an initial exploration of the text at home.

If a longer text is not something you can listen to, read, or view completely in class or is not available on the Internet, you need to make the text available to students in your school's learning center or library. By the same token, if Internet access is essential, try to make technology available for this purpose. By letting students have an initial experience with a longer text on their own, they can have their second LEO-focused interaction with peers in class.

In classes where nonprint texts are a primary focus (a class focusing on film, text literacy, art or music history, consumer sciences, a community garden, or digital production), you will probably use more, and also longer, texts; we think these types of courses can also benefit from shorter texts as this allows for a focus on depth over breadth. We will give more examples of this philosophy in the possibilities section.

> Our first *Kit Kittredge* clip is slightly over three minutes long. With students this simple clip might be played three times coupled with fifty minutes of individual and collaborative exploration and discussion. With adults the same clip can be used for thirty to fifty minutes of discussion.

Step 4: Prep and Assemble Materials

Once you choose LEOs to scaffold your text, make sure to photocopy or download and print the LEOs. As you and your students become comfortable with a wider range of LEOs, you will want to copy or print enough so that students have an excess of LEOs to choose from. Save those that students do not choose/use for another learning experience. We strongly recommend using different colors of paper for different LEOs; students are more efficient with their learning cues if we ask them to find a certain color of paper, as opposed to rifling through ten sheets of white paper.

If you can't color code the LEOs, the next best thing is to write different numbers at the top of each LEO before you copy them. That way they can be referenced quickly during your first LEO-based learning experiences. Being organized makes the experience time-responsive and allows for the richest use of instructional time. **We suggest that you wait until after step 5 to distribute LEOs to students.**

If your texts require preparation, cue them up, tear out the pages (we love using used books with photos, maps, infographics, or artwork), and test your projectors, speakers, and whatever technology you are using to share your texts. Technology glitches are a frustrating starting point for any learning experience. Many texts are available on the Internet. If access is a challenge, perhaps you can create a wiki page or work with a school text specialist to make the materials easily accessible to students onsite before and after school.

It is always a smart practice to have extra pencils, pens, crayons, colored pencils, or markers available. If you decide to have groups synthesize and share their discussions (see step 8), this could be done with markers on chart paper. You might also supply group folders, paper clips, or small binder clips to organize the groups' work each day. It depends on your goals.

> When we workshop *Kit Kittredge*, each LEO is on a separate sheet of colored paper. We use those colors to organize learners throughout our learning experience. At the end of the day we can collect them in color sets (e.g., one pink, blue, purple, and yellow) or, if we are doing groups based on LEOs, we can group or collect "all the people with pink sheets" or quickly create "rainbow groups" where you join a group where each person has a different colored LEO.

Step 5: Introduce the Text(s)

It is best for students to experience a text once, without LEOs or too much background or instruction. This sets a rich stage for students to generate questions and places for inquiry. If you like to tell students what questions, objectives, or standards are being covered at the beginning you can, but we prefer to address those things at the end of a learning experience, after things have been uncovered by groups of students. Students' initial reading allows them to get their bearings and develop some initial ideas or questions about the text without worrying about what they feel they should be doing as they read a text.

Before students interact with whatever text you're using, give quick orientations containing just enough background knowledge, vocabulary, and whatever else is needed to get them to a place to make meaning and connections. Again, it is generally more powerful for them to uncover that information. Remember, the point of LEOs is for students to uncover information collaboratively, so don't overdo your explanation. Reflect on how you scaffold to meet the needs of your particular goals and let the learning experience begin.

> If your text is an audio or video excerpt, try thinking like a talk-show host and set up the basics of the clip with a small anecdote or prologue to orient students to the work. For *Kit Kittredge,* do your best talk show host impersonation and say something like this:

"The clip you're going to see is from the film *Kit Kittredge: An American Girl*, and it takes place during the time known as the Great Depression. Before this clip Kit's father leaves Cincinnati because he wants to find work in Chicago. This leaves Kit, an aspiring reporter, and her mother to manage things in Ohio. We're going to be working with this clip for the next two days, and I'll give you more specific information over time. For now just enjoy the clip."

Step 6: Assign, Distribute, and Model LEOs

When you initiate the practice of using LEOs with your students, you will likely need to start by modeling sample responses for the entire class. As mentioned in step 2, we recommend modeling a minimum of two LEOs before you expect students to do them solo. We have also had success when students uncover how LEOs work in groups—but when you first do the practice we think it is worth elaborating on this because you have many options moving forward.

With fifty-five LEOs to choose from—plus any you might create—you can develop a repertoire over time. Mixing them up keeps the practice fresh and furthers differentiation and engagement. As you and your students become more familiar with different types of texts and LEOs, your curriculum will pop more (become more efficient, effective, fun, and engaged) over the course of a school year.

When you're beginning you might have the whole class do one LEO together in the traditional "read a text and fill out the study guide" fashion. If a previous class has used LEOs, you might bring completed LEOs from this class, or even have former students model them with your new group of students. As you'll see in step 8, choosing to start with at least two LEOs will allow you to practice collaborative learning experiences more easily. When students get comfortable, they can begin to self-select LEOs. You can create three- to five-student groups at this point and lay out eight LEOs for students to choose from. Three to five LEOs will be selected. We do not recommend a choice among the fifty-five LEOs, but rather suggest that you (or a group of students) preselect seven or eight LEOs that work with the texts being used.

If you are doing a text over multiple days (like a feature film), then students can choose a LEO for each day they work with the text (e.g., if you plan to work with a text for four days, then each student should engage in four of the eight LEOs, with four discarded). Over time the LEO selection process evolves into a fun and social learning event. What usually happens is that students have a definite LEO that they think will work better or be more interesting with different kinds of texts. The LEOs become students' footprints of learning and qualitative data you can share with your colleagues and administrators to show evidence of student participation and learning.

After students have their third experience with LEOs, you will likely need to spend less time on expository information as it becomes integrated into your classroom culture. Once this happens you have more options for how students distribute and select LEOs.

When we use *Kit Kittredge* with new audiences, we model in more subtle ways. If we have twenty-four students in the class, we pass out six copies of each of four LEOs: Fashion Critic, Tech Specialist, Economist, and Wordsmith. Because this is a first encounter with LEOs, we distribute them randomly; we don't offer choice just yet.

We briefly explain the LEO procedure to give students the big picture. We keep the directions simple, saying something like this:

"We're going to be working with the clip you just watched for the next two days. You will re-watch the *Kit Kittredge* clip today one or two more times. You have been given a Learning Experience Organizer (called a LEO for short) that asks you to have a specific viewing focus as you work with the text. Many of your peers will be looking at different details. After we have revisited the text a few times, you will share findings with your classmates.

"Please take a few minutes to read the directions at the top of the LEO and write down any questions you might want to ask about your LEO before we re-watch the clip."

After about two minutes, we remind students to write down their questions and open the floor up for a handful of questions. Students usually ask the questions you would have liked to cover. They ask for clarification and create spaces for you to share sample LEO responses, ideas, or tips related to their questions.

After answering students' questions, we explain that we will circulate in the classroom to help out after re-watching the clip. This allows spaces for us to model as needed. It saves time, encourages students to interact more thoughtfully with the LEOs, and allows for more personalized instruction.

Step 7: Revisit Texts and Create Time for Individual LEO Exploration

After you assign or students choose LEOs, explain to students that "we will be viewing/watching /looking/reading/listening to the text again individually." Making time for individual exploration is an essential element to set up successful collaboration. We rarely put students in groups right away because this makes it easy for individual students to opt out of discussion by leaning on their peers' ideas.

The time you allow for this step depends largely on the type and length of a text. If you were working with a series of images like advertisements, artworks, or photos, you might spread the images on the classroom floor in step 5 and have students look carefully at the images for three minutes. After the initial viewing time you can ask students to choose an image they think is interesting. That will be the image they will explore with the help of a LEO.

For audio, video, and print texts, your individual LEO exploration time will increase in relation to the length of the text.

> In the case of *Kit Kittredge* we explain:
>
> "We will view the clip a second time. Be sure to watch carefully using the focus on your LEO. After we show the clip again you will have individual time to complete your LEO. During that time we will play the clip a third time, with the volume turned down a bit, in case you need to catch some more details."
>
> This sequence, including the two reviewings, usually takes ten to fifteen minutes.

Step 8: Group Students and Facilitate Discussion

Before you decide the type of groups you will create, the more practical issue is the size of groups. Having three to five students per group is the best way to facilitate learning. We almost always recommend creating as many groups as possible, as this allows for more active learning, discussion, and individual participation. If you have attendance challenges at your school, you might want to have groups of four or five instead of three. When there are too few people in a group—particularly when one is absent—conversation can stagnate.

After students complete their individual LEOs around a text, there are many effective ways to group them for collaboration. We first like to create groups where people with the same LEO get together. We call these **shared LEO groups.** This initial group allows students to collaboratively develop a wider range of responses before they join what we call **mixed LEO groups.** (If you don't have time for shared LEO groups, you can skip to the mixed groups right away.)

Beginning with shared LEO groups helps students build on their individual ideas and observations and add information noted by other students. We find the shared groups to be helpful and fun for kids because they yield a lot of "a-ha" moments. We hear a lot of statements like, "Wow, I totally missed that" or "That was a cool point!"

> Making time for individual exploration is an essential element to set up successful collaboration.

Here, students who may have struggled with a LEO for whatever reason are given additional opportunities to expand their ideas and thinking. This also makes it less likely that a student will feel inadequate going to the mixed group with minimal reflection. Again, this is differentiated, not simply because each student has a different LEO task, but because a student who struggles with one of the skills on a LEO can learn from peers.

The collaboration that LEOs support becomes a great way to model the adage "it is not how smart you are, but how you are smart." The shared groups make the entire learning experience less intimidating and more successful for a wider range of learners.

During both the shared and mixed groups, listen carefully to your students as they work; talk, coach, model, and read their work and help them craft multiple responses to texts. When LEOs are a part of your practice and students are comfortable with them, you'll find that the students will push their peers toward more reflective and metacognitive thinking on a regular basis.

Doing steps 5, 6, and 7 and allowing about ten minutes for this shared group usually takes up a standard fifty-minute class period. If this is your breaking point for the first day, take a look at step 9 where we talk about pausing your learning experience. Of course, your initial LEO experiences might take more time. Even after developing your practice, interesting discoveries and conversations can take additional time.

After completing the first shared LEO grouping, you can ask students to create mixed LEO groups of four where each LEO is represented—if you color code you can call these "rainbow groups." Students don't always remember all the LEO names initially. For that reason we usually have an overhead, posterboard, or digital projection of the four colors of the sheets in a square for quick reference (e.g., one pink, blue, purple, and yellow). This simple visual saves a lot of time. Again, if you have not color-coded the sheets, you can number each sheet as explained in step 4. Then you can create groups with one of each number 1 through 4.

In these mixed LEO groups each student shares his or her LEO and experiences the other three LEOs in far more detail. In this way the process resembles the classic jigsaw puzzle, with each student bringing a piece to the table to create a fuller understanding of the text. After allowing about ten to fifteen minutes for this discussion, you can ask students to capture the most interesting points from each group to share with the class.

We listen in the small-group setting and in the debriefing (large-group setting). We then encourage one member of each group to speak for the group. We and other students pose questions and listen to comments that help us understand whether students are "getting it."

You might do this part by giving each group a sheet of chart paper and markers and asking students to share one question, a quote from the group, and an interesting idea. This keeps them critically focused on their discussion.

Another option (and this is a great one to use if you have some students who join the learning experience later in the class period or miss a day of class) is to hand out one of the LEOs designed to help collect and summarize the group work for any given day (like the Producer, Summarizer, or Archivist LEOs) and have someone capture the group's thoughts on that LEO before sharing with the whole group.

After each group synthesizes their LEOs through discussion, you can have a group pair share (where one group shares with another) or have all groups share with the larger group. We find that the most exciting outcome of this shared to mixed LEO grouping sequence is the collegial and collaborative spaces it creates. These flexible structures help students rise to the occasion and make fascinating connections and contributions.

In our *Kit Kittredge* example there were four LEOs distributed to twenty-four students, with six students doing each LEO. If you have color-coded the LEOs, you can simply ask for all the pinks, greens, or blues to form groups in different corners of the room. If LEOs are on white paper, you can do this grouping by LEO titles or numbers. From there you could split each group of six in half or leave this slightly larger grouping.

Step 9: Pause or End the Day's LEO-Based Learning Experience

As noted in step 8, your learning experience may end at a convenient place, or it may not. If groups or the class is midstream or completing their learning experience, you have many options. You can:

- let students work until the class period ends and collect sheets in progress.

- use sticky notes as exit slips on which students list something they learned or a question they had about their learning experience thus far.

- use sticky notes as exit slips to have students make suggestions on how their group might improve their work.

- ask group leaders to collect LEOs until your next session.

- hand out Group Evaluation LEOs (see step 10) and have students peer-assess each other's work and participation.

Additionally, you can post your essential questions, objectives, or standards on the board and ask groups to be metacognitive by answering how this learning experience related to those goals. Those observations can be written up on chart paper and shared with the whole class. This type of activity usually works better when you're completing the experience.

> In our *Kit Kittredge* example we usually ask students to reflect on what they learned about the Great Depression and ask them to support those claims with evidence from the film as we're using this to support close readings of text and building background knowledge.

Step 10: Assess the LEO-Based Learning Experiences

LEOs can be assessed in many ways, depending on the standard or goal that you are trying to achieve. Our suggestion is to work with these models and include the goal or standard that you are working with in class. You can develop the rubric in any way that shows student understanding. Following are a standards-based example and a simple point-based rubric. These are simply examples that can be adjusted to meet your needs. You also can use more than one goal or standard to suit the opportunity for learning. Remember, too, that you can use the Group Evaluation pages (standard and point-based versions) as another option.

Example Rubrics

Standards-Based Reading Standard 7 CCSS.ELA-LITERACY.CCRA.R.7
The learner will integrate and evaluate content presented in diverse formats and media, including visually and quantitatively, as well as in words.

EXCEEDS STANDARD	ABOVE STANDARD	MEETS STANDARD	MEETS STANDARD WITH HELP	DOES NOT MEET STANDARD
The learner integrated and evaluated (with appropriate support, connections, *and* examples) content presented in diverse formats and media, including visually and quantitatively, as well as in words.	The learner integrated and evaluated (with appropriate support) content presented in diverse formats and media, including visually and quantitatively, as well as in words.	The learner integrated and evaluated content presented in diverse formats and media, including visually and quantitatively, as well as in words.	With help, the learner was able to either integrate *or* evaluate content presented in diverse formats and media, including visually *or* quantitatively as well as in words.	The learner was unable to integrate and evaluate content presented in diverse formats and media, including visually and quantitatively, as well as in words.

Points-Based Reading Standard 7 CCSS.ELA-LITERACY.CCRA.R.7
The learner will integrate and evaluate content presented in diverse formats and media, including visually and quantitatively, as well as in words.

INNOVATING 3	EMERGING 2	DEVELOPING 1
The learner integrated and evaluated (with appropriate support, connections, *and* examples) content presented in diverse formats and media, including visually and quantitatively, as well as in words.	The learner integrated and evaluated content presented in diverse formats and media, including visually and quantitatively, as well as in words.	With help, the learner was able to either integrate *or* evaluate content presented in diverse formats and media, including visually *or* quantitatively as well as in words.

Using LEOs to make your curriculum pop is a process of continuous assessment. We make it our responsibility to communicate with students in oral, written, and numerical forms (quantitative and qualitative feedback) at different points of their LEO experience.

Many schools talk about being data driven, but these efforts are usually applied to more traditional quantitative assessments. LEOs, though, can be quantitatively assessed if this is essential in your learning community. Most LEOs are designed for many possible responses, so we often assess these footprints of learning based on process and effort.

- Did the students fill out the LEO to the best of their ability?

- Do they have any unique and original observations?

- Was there a clear effort to use the class time?

When your LEO-based learning experiences come together, you will be able to "eyeball" student LEOs, giving a majority of students full credit/points and spending your time responding to an interesting idea or two on their documents.

As mentioned in step 9, you can also do simple peer evaluations to assess contributions within their small groups. These points can be in place of individual LEO grades or a complement to them. Neither of us is overly concerned about punishment and rewards, but we do find that peer assessments can be a useful tool to help students stay on task.

Because peers are assessing peers, it adds a collaborative dimension to their assessment as participants assign points to the members of the group using the standards and point-based Group Evaluation LEOs. These LEOs are included because it makes students accountable rather than having teachers as the ultimate judges of student effort and work. Each student can individually fill out the Group Evaluation LEO, or you can have students verbally work through a single evaluation LEO page for the whole group. You can even have each student fill out a new evaluation LEO every day you work with the tools. If you're not yet comfortable with peer evaluation, you can always be a participant in groups' evaluation process.

This simple rubric is something you can always modify to fit your needs and goals. We would collect those peer-evaluated LEOs and double-check the accuracy of those assessments.

Peer evaluations, LEOs, and every option listed in step 9 would most commonly be used as formative assessments because they are part of a larger learning experience ending with some summative assessments. In some classes a summative assessment means a traditional multiple-choice test. In our classes this is usually a differentiated or authentic project. Either way, most LEO experiences are usually steps on a longer journey.

Also, any notes you might collect while observing students participating in collaboration around LEOs also fall into the category of formative assessments. These are all footprints of learning and data to be considered. You can also use LEOs as summative assessments. We will give an example of this in Chapter 3.

LEOs are designed to create spaces for all teachers and students to learn. Designing these types of learning experiences means that teachers are holding up their end of the student-teacher collaboration.

In our *Kit Kittredge* example we usually have students share out in large groups, collect the LEOs, and assess based on in-class participation and the criteria mentioned previously:

- Did the students fill out the LEO to the best of their abilities?

- Do they have any unique and original observations?

- Was there a clear effort to use the class time?

CHAPTER 3

POSSIBILITIES, MODIFICATIONS, AND MODELS

We want to remind you that there is no single right way to use LEOs—there are better ways, but a lot depends on your needs, the needs of students, and the choices and modifications you make. The procedure explained in Chapter 2 is a starting point. This chapter will offer ideas for how to make LEOs a part of your unique classroom cultures.

LEOs: Outcomes of a Flexible Structure

Whether the whole class explores a short clip (like those from *Kit Kittredge*) or each student looks at different texts (as highlighted in the following possibilities), LEO-based learning experiences allow students to discover content, patterns, and connections through a wide range of texts. LEOs can be the starting points for students to design wiki pages or other digital presentations where they showcase multimodal texts and ask other students to explore texts and LEOs they select.

LEOs let our students know that, while working with text is fun, it also carries with it the responsibility to understand, interpret, and use critical thinking skills to make meanings. We offer the LEOs as a way for students to take a more focused and thoughtful look at what a text says and does.

For example, when viewing a film without the structure of LEOs, our students might tell us that the characters wore "funny-looking clothes," but little else. Using LEOs, students generally go beyond a simplistic description because the LEO criteria suggest ways to look at fashion in the film with more attention to detail. Questions and prompts for more reflection direct the students' thinking by asking them to think about the "why"; they take notes on the LEO page and on a portion of the image, object, space, clip, infographic, film, music, article, or other text. We view these close reading skills as an important component of reflection.

When we began using diverse LEOs in our classes, we saw an immediate difference in how students interacted with texts. If you simply ask students to take notes, they might write down what the teacher is saying or copy topic sentences from a textbook. LEOs—especially those with unique ways of seeing—help students focus on their individual thinking and synthesis of text. For that reason, we always find students referring to their notes on the LEOs to reinforce thinking and discussion.

Because LEO notes are usually processed multiple times in small groups, students' ideas are more thought provoking and refined when they enter a full-class discussion. Students are able to articulate thoughts about what they saw, read, and/or heard, and they usually retain that information for a much longer time. This is deep and socially constructed reading at its strongest, because it is done collaboratively.

LEOs are highly engaging, especially for students who are not regular participants in classroom discussions. We hypothesize that these students become involved for a variety of reasons:

○ They can socialize.

○ They can participate in a way that allows their voices to be heard.

○ They can showcase their understanding of the text in a safe environment.

○ They only have to focus on one LEO about the text during "reading."

○ They realize that there are multiple "better answers," so they don't worry as much about getting the "wrong answer." They think!

Like any human endeavor, we only improve if we do things regularly, with deliberate practice. One rarely gets healthier by dieting for just one week, or fitter by running for a single day. If your classroom culture already encourages spaces for many "better answers" (as opposed to singular right answers) and collaborative learning, integrating LEOs might be easy.

In most cases it takes time to regularly make your curriculum pop using LEOs. It takes time, experimentation, and repetition. If they are used regularly, LEOs scaffold learning so that students understand texts more deeply. When a critic looks at a film, she has critical theory or a base for understanding what to look at and how to measure what she has seen using standards or criteria. LEOs become a frame of reference that supports the critical study of any text.

> LEOs let our students know that, while working with text is fun, it also carries with it the responsibility to understand, interpret, and use critical thinking skills to make meanings.

Also, while we believe that these are a strong structure for learning experiences, we also believe there is no single way to make your curriculum pop with LEOs—they are a flexible structure. By way of metaphor, even a massive skyscraper like the Sears (now Willis) Tower in Chicago is made of materials that allow it to sway in the wind. If it were not designed with "wiggle room," it would collapse. Similarly, consider the LEO structures offered here as raw materials for you to build on and manipulate in order to make your curriculum pop.

Possibilities

In Chapter 2, we modeled LEOs using short clips from *Kit Kittredge*, exploring a single film clip (from a choice of two) with the entire class. Whole-class instruction is a great way to use LEOs, but you can also have groups or individuals explore multiple texts. During that process we mentioned that an almost infinite number of texts could have been used to explore our working content objective. Our goal for that model was to develop students' close reading skills while developing background knowledge about the Great Depression and how it affected the daily lives of Americans. Let's look at some other ways you could tackle this objective with different short texts. We'll start with some suggested texts by text type and suggest some small-group and whole-group options for each.

Artwork

One of the most famous Works Progress Administration (WPA) murals was created by Mexican artist Diego Rivera and is currently at the Detroit Institute of Art (DIA). Their website (dia.org/art/rivera-court.aspx) has some excellent reproductions of this massive artwork. Each student can look at different sections of the mural using a wide range of LEOs to make meanings built around your objectives.

Students can explore WPA posters produced from 1936 to 1943 (loc.gov/pictures/collection/wpapos). Groups or individual students could each explore a poster or a collection of posters. They could view these texts on a device or you could print color reproductions for classroom use. Each student can look at a text or texts with different LEOs and share information about common themes and findings around Depression-era culture in shared and mixed LEO groups.

The same procedure and options could be used with the Library of Congress's online exhibitions "Documenting America: Photographic Series," "Life of the People: Realist Prints and Drawings from the Ben and Beatrice Goldstein Collection, 1912–1948," or the "Bound for Glory: 1939–1943" photo collection.

Incorporating the LEOs linked to visual texts like Body Linguist, Highlighter, Intuitor, and Sensor could be helpful here.

Radio Programs

In 2000, National Public Radio (NPR) ran a piece by the Kitchen Sisters titled "Voices from the Dust Bowl—Lost and Found Sound: The Recordings of Todd and Sonkin" (available for free online). The whole class could listen to these oral histories utilizing LEOs such as Timeliner, Visualizer, or Web Master.

You could also do a whole-class exploration of an exemplary radio show from the 1930s like Orson Welles's "War of the Worlds" broadcast, or students could each choose an old radio program as listening homework. You can preselect a series of shows from archive.org (archive.org/details /oldtimeradio), purchase a sampler of shows from the time period at Radio Spirits (radiospirits.com), or find free podcasts on iTunes (do an Internet search for "iTunes old time radio" and you'll see a wide range of free podcasts available for download).

You can present six to eight shows to students as listening options— different episodes of the same show or shows representing different radio genres (news, comedy, drama, etc.). If you want to use shorter audio texts, you can find collections of thirty-second radio ads from the 1930s.

Comics

Find 1930s comic strips (*Krazy Kat, Dick Tracy, Little Orphan Annie, The Yellow Kid,* or *Buck Rogers*) or political cartoons. You can also excerpt graphic novels set in the 1930s, such as *Kings in Disguise* by Dan Burr and James Vance; *Satchel Paige: Striking Out Jim Crow* by James Sturm and Rich Tommaso; *Woody Guthrie and the Dust Bowl Ballads* by Nick Hayes, or *The Storm in the Barn* by Matt Phelan.

Books

Purchase a used copy of a classic Great Depression oral history collection like Studs Terkel's *Hard Times.* Tear the book up and do a jigsaw exercise in which individual students study different pages—either from selected interviews or chosen at random from all over the text—and then come together to teach one another about what they have learned.

With this example, the case can be made that students are exploring multiple texts (different stories/people/histories) or that they're actually exploring a whole text. Either way, LEOs can be used to draw connections and parallels between the excerpted texts. You can also use excerpts from popular children's books (start by looking up the 1930s Caldecott Award winners).

Music

Technological advances in sound recording and the advent of affordable radios boosted the music industry during the Depression. You could design a whole-class LEOs experience around an exemplary song from the period like Woody Guthrie's "This Land Is Your Land" (making sure to use the oft-excluded, critical verses[18]) or Billie Holiday's track, "Strange Fruit."[19]

---

18. For more information on "This Land Is Your Land," see the Rock and Roll Hall of Fame and Museum Lesson Plan titled "STI Lesson 9—Woody Guthrie and *The Grapes of Wrath*" (rockhall.com/education/resources/lesson-plans).
19. For more on the history of this song, see billieholiday.com/portfolio/strange-fruit.

With popular music you might begin using multiple texts for your LEOs experience. You could select a series of songs for individual and/or small-group exploration. Period artists include Bessie Smith, Ma Rainey, Mahalia Jackson, Robert Johnson, Louis Armstrong, Benny Goodman, Ella Fitzgerald, Billie Holiday, the Carter Family, and Bob Wills. You might also highlight the work of songwriters like Irving Berlin and George Gershwin as performed by stars like Bing Crosby and Judy Garland. LEOs such as the Poet, Visualizer, or Moodcatcher come in handy with music texts.

Whether you choose to focus on an individual text (song) or multiple texts, be sure students can access songs and song lyrics in class or online via a word processing document with hyperlinks or a simple webpage (like Google sites), or share your links via your Learning Management System (like Edmodo or Schoology).

Museums

The Library of Congress has a vast digital collection of primary source texts available to the public. Their webpage "The Great Depression Exhibition and Presentations" is a springboard for the ideas that follow.

Cultural Artifacts

In the spirit of a great book by Neil MacGregor called *A History of the World in 100 Objects*, we can look at technological innovations of the time. A basic Internet image search for "1930s technology" will give you links to products that were introduced during the decade. You could put examples or photos of things like frozen food, Scotch tape, chocolate chip cookies, parking meters, the game Monopoly, radar, or a ballpoint pen at different group workstations for students to explore with LEOs.

Ecology Texts

You can also examine spaces or ecosystems. You might compare land use and populations in the 1930s to the present day. The National Institute of Food and Agriculture (NIFA) and the United States Department of Agriculture (USDA) have a multimedia website called "Growing a Nation" that explores agriculture (population and land use) over time. There you can access their 1930 timeline and compare it to their 1990–2000 timeline; both give statistics on the United States' total population, farm populations, average acres, and farm income. You might also explore the U.S. Census Bureau population distribution maps over time and growth and distribution of cities maps from 1790 to 2000.

These are all ways to look at land and land usage as a text. In the wake of Ken Burns's *Dust Bowl* documentary on PBS, we were hoping there would be a "then vs. now" coffee-table book of photography. While that text does not seem to exist, we did find a wonderful series of videos from OETA (the Oklahoma PBS Network) on YouTube and the Oklahoma Conservation Commission's website that explores "lessons from the Dust Bowl." Each short segment shows the different ways people are cultivating land-scapes to avoid the ecological problems that were at the heart of the Great Depression.

Infographics

If you want to tap into logical/mathematical intelligences around our objective, search phrases like "1930s by the numbers" or "infographics about the 1930s." The Weather Channel website even has a data comparison "The Dust Bowl: 2012 vs. 1930s." You can also find a plethora of graphs charting income inequality over the last 150 years. This gets you started on a wide range of numerical representations from, of, and about the era.

You could distribute one set of statistics and graphs to the whole class or distribute different data sets to groups or individuals. You could start with LEOs designed for math (like Cryptographer, Data Analyst, or X-cavator) and incorporate those that seem suited to the humanities (like Sociologist or Demographer). There are myriad ways to do numerical analysis that help students attach mathematical symbols to larger story lines.

Architecture

We live outside Chicago, a city rich with architectural history. Ideally, it would be great to take a field trip to a collection of buildings from the 1930s and have students use LEOs in those settings, but another possibility is to go to the Chicago Historical Society and collect/print photos of famous Frank Lloyd Wright homes, prefabricated bungalows built en masse outside the city center, and larger buildings like the Crow Island School in the Chicago suburb of Winnetka (considered one of the great American buildings of the 1930s) for students to explore. And if you don't live near Chicago, you can explore your city or go "virtual" to find artifacts or buildings online from your location.

Websites

To focus on the digital domain for this objective, you might first create a learning experience and design a follow-up experience that makes thematic collections using current websites. The post-2008 crash economy dubbed the

Great Recession produced the Tea Party movement, Occupy Wall Street, and tent cities. Have students analyze Twitter streams with #occupywallstreet or #teaparty hashtags; search for the Great Depression or Great Recession on Flickr or Tumblr to find images; or search the *New York Times* and *Wall Street Journal*'s online archives (nice ideological opposites) that deal with the effects of the recession (school budget cuts, job losses, etc.).

There are also wonderful nonfiction texts on the Web that connect past and present. The *New York Times* Learning Network has a lesson from 2008 titled "A Tale of Two Leaders" that compares the challenges faced by FDR in the 1930s to those faced by Obama in 2008. This lesson includes many supplemental texts (including data sets).

Also (and this could also be part of an ecological exploration), in the wake of Ken Burns's *Dust Bowl* documentary, many major magazines ran articles exploring current droughts to those of the Great Depression: see "Are We Headed for Another Dust Bowl?" on Smithsonian.com and "Parched: A New Dust Bowl Forms in the Heartland" at Nationalgeographic.com. Additionally, California's recent megadrought is being referred to as "California's Dust Bowl" by the *LA Times*. All these online texts give rich areas of exploration and comparison related to our objective.

Films

Returning to our *Kit Kittredge* model, the whole class does not have to view this clip. You can use a diverse series of YouTube or DVD film clips that have portions set in the 1930s or which were created in the Great Depression. Options include Chaplin's *Hard Times* (1936), *The Natural* (1984), *Amelia* (2009), *King Kong* (2005), *Citizen Kane* (1941), *Me and Orson Welles* (2009), *Radio Days* and *Malcolm X* (1992), *To Kill a Mockingbird* (1962), *Lady Sings the Blues* (1972), *O Brother, Where Art Thou?* (2000), *Angela's Ashes* (1999), or *Cinderella Man* (2005).

A longer full-class text might include a viewing of *The Grapes of Wrath* (1940) or large portions of Ken Burns's documentary *Dust Bowl* (2012) and its accompanying website (pbs.org/kenburns/dustbowl).

Mindfully selected LEOs will likely reveal a lot about the era of any film's creation. As mentioned earlier, you might have students choose four LEOs (from a set of eight) and use a different one for every day of viewing.

Final Thoughts on LEO Possibilities

Whatever texts you choose and however you decide to use the LEOs, it is always smart when possible to prepare your texts in collaboration with your professional learning community, department team, or school media specialists or teaching librarians. These experts can assist you and your students with the creation of online galleries or wikis collecting texts. They can also help you access and print digital or microfilm texts to share offline in your classroom.

From *Kit Kittredge* through all the LEOs possibilities listed here, you will find that any of these multimodal, differentiated learning experiences can help make your curriculum pop. Rich, intriguing, and unusual texts engage more students and allow them to explore more content than they would have by simply reading a textbook and filling out traditional study guides.

In Chapter 2, we talked about the many ways you can assess LEO-based learning experiences. There, we primarily focused on using LEOs to do formative assessment. You can also use LEOs as part of a group summative assessment around your skill or content objective. You could give students excerpts or short texts that they have explored during the course of your larger unit (a political cartoon, a graph, a short story, radio ad, textbook excerpt, an online video). From there you could give students four LEOs each and ask them to individually reflect on their texts using two LEOs. Then you can creatively group students to have them uncover big ideas and themes from the larger unit. You can grade this work as a collaborative summative assessment on the unit.

Modifications and Models

Experience has shown us that the LEOs usually work with a wide range of middle school, secondary, college, and adult learners. Many groups have the same challenges; things like vocabulary can be an issue even for graduate students. We are always interested in unusual or interesting words. For example, many students will not know what a demographer or sociologist might do, but the LEOs present ample context clues about their meanings. When students meet in shared LEO groups, they tend to uncover these meanings.

Remember, students don't have to know the meaning of every word or phrase because they can discover these things during the learning experience. We also find that the choice and flexibility of the LEOs usually do a nice job of connecting reluctant readers with texts. They don't have to panic about being wrong when there are so many ways to be right.

However, there are three likely possibilities where you might need to modify or design new LEOs:

1. You might want to alter the LEO text for some specific purpose. We strongly discourage making any of the LEOs so specific that they resemble a traditional study guide (designed for narrow, singular answers),

but we encourage people to tweak the LEOs to suit their needs. See the chart on locking and interlocking study guides in Chapter 1.

2. You might imagine a LEO not collected in this book. Again, we encourage you to develop new LEOs for texts that you are exploring. When creating new LEOs, be sure to think about Bloom's Taxonomy (caveats from Chapter 1 included), Webb's Depth of Knowledge, or Costa's Levels of Questioning (popularized as the Three-Story Intellect) to help you design for open-ended, student-centered thinking.

3. Though LEOs generally engage and accommodate a wide range of student interests, learning styles, and abilities, there are situations where you might work with special-needs populations, ELL/ESL populations, or those with significant learning challenges that require further scaffolding. You might also be interested in modifying the LEOs for K–3 elementary students by altering vocabulary or simplifying focuses. The following figures show more basic LEOs that can maintain the spirit of the LEOs in Chapter 5 for these populations.

Figure 3.1 Model A LEO: Special Needs or Grades K–3

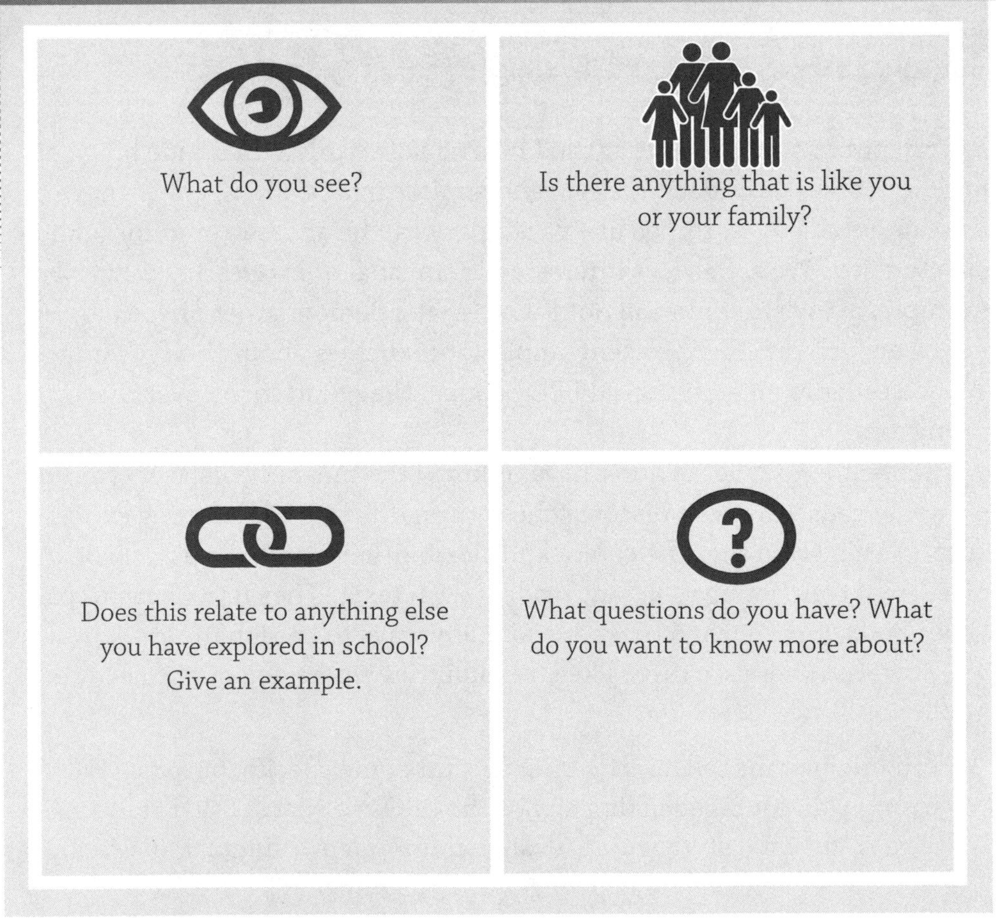

What do you see?

Is there anything that is like you or your family?

Does this relate to anything else you have explored in school? Give an example.

What questions do you have? What do you want to know more about?

Assign one square to a group of four students.

Figure 3.2 Model B LEO: Special Needs or Grades 4–6

Who/what are the people
or things in the text?

What do you see, hear,
or think about?

Do you have any connections
to the text?

Does this relate to anything else
you've explored in school?
Give an example?

What question do you have
about the text?

Are there any words you do not
understand or are curious about?

What are comments or quotes of
interest from the text?

Suggestions for a Positive LEO Experience

Here are some common issues and suggestions that can help achieve a positive and full learning experience.

CHALLENGE	Suggestions
Off-task behavior/ digression	Choose texts that allow for many responses. Students like to feel successful; actually, most people like to feel successful, so consider the LEOs that allow for challenging students.
Uneven participation	Model the text adequately before you begin, based on the ability level of your students. You may have to model discussion to encourage as fair and even participation as possible. There are talkers and there are those who say little. See the details on this in Chapter 2, step 2.
Quick finish/ robotic LEO discussion	Choose richer texts. Vary the LEOs. LEOs can get dull if you choose the same LEOs and type of texts repeatedly. Don't let your practice get stale; use texts and LEOs that stretch you and your students to enjoy learning. Rich texts are ones that make students curious—as such, they often exhibit novelty, complexity, ambiguity, and variety.
Students want to watch/view/ read/hear/ explore the full text.	You may have to train students to be comfortable with excerpts and shorter texts. Shorter class periods lend themselves easily to using shorter texts.
Students complete individual or group work early.	We always suggest that students take a second or third look at their work. Students sometimes skip over vital information to finish their work and socialize; remind them that they are accountable for their work. This is one reason why we created the LEOs and rubrics for daily participation and written work: so students participate meaningfully in the LEO-based learning experience.
Students get frustrated.	Sometimes students are comfortable with classroom activities that emphasize single right answers and individual performance. Often, these students are not comfortable working in groups and do not like the gray nature of LEOs. Other students, however, *do* like the discovery and open-ended discussion that LEOs allow. As a great teacher, it is your call to work with both learning preferences to allow for optimum understanding and to differentiate for various learning styles. Keep in mind Carol Dweck's research and work with students toward a growth mindset.

Putting It All Together

When you learned to ride a bike, you probably used training wheels or had someone running alongside holding you as you pedaled. Think of this book as your training wheels: read and reread our text for new ideas. Ask students about their successes and challenges with LEOs on quick sticky-note exit slips. Don't feel pressured to ditch the practice because a single student is confused; ask what is confusing and modify your practice as needed. We continually work at making our curriculum pop and anticipate that learning experiences that flop will lead to a higher percentage of those that pop.

Cooperative learning experiences designed around LEOs are designed to structure, not to be magic. LEOs don't create significant learning experiences without the mindful experimentation and practice by great teachers. Keep in mind that LEOs are flexible structures with plenty of room for your students to showcase their understanding of texts. Modeling, repeating, experiencing, verbalizing, and socializing help create a powerful learning experience.

We have found that our curriculum pops when students have more opportunities to interact and collaborate with classmates using LEOs. The LEOs foci create a learning atmosphere that promotes individual contributions and creates an excellent space for what computer programmers might call "peer to peer networking" or what academics might refer to as "participatory culture" or "socially constructed learning."

CHAPTER 4

RESOURCES TO MAKE YOUR CURRICULUM POP

With such a wide range of texts and LEOs to choose from, many teachers ask us for ideas to begin their practice. To those ends, we offer multiple points of entry around some major text categories.

This chapter has four purposes reflected in the variety of the resources:

1. To help you choose LEOs that go beyond the basics of the Archivist, Connector, Highlighter, Summarizer, Visualizer, Wonderer, and Wordsmith to get you started in each text type.

2. To provide you with suggestions for using Twitter as a social text resource to help you keep current on present trends, teaching ideas, and people related to each text type.

3. To guide you in locating books, websites, and movies that familiarize you with the text in question. Selections are not comprehensive but are designed to give you a sense of the history, practice, and culture, as well as rationales for educational uses of each text.

4. To encourage you in finding teachable texts of any type.

First, we have suggested that the basic LEOs to get you started are those most closely related to traditional literature circles practices. As you start using LEOs, we suggest beginning with LEOs like Archivist, Connector, Highlighter, Summarizer, Visualizer, Wonderer, and Wordsmith, as these are the most familiar types of inquiry that work with the widest range of texts.

In this resource section we go beyond those basics to suggest LEOs that can be easily applied in a variety of text categories. As you build groups of three to five students, you want to give students a choice among eight LEOs, though the group will use only four to five of them; students enjoy choosing LEOs that are appealing or challenging, based on their individual needs. You can use the following texts as initial suggestions and work toward a larger palette of LEOs that include some of your own creation.

Second, we believe that most educators can benefit from using Twitter as part of their professional learning network. At the top of each section we have included Twitter hashtags. These hashtags (starting with a #) are designed to help you follow ideas and resources on any given topic. This is an excellent place for you to connect with other practitioners and to learn about emerging trends and educational applications for rich texts.

You don't need a Twitter account to search; you can go to twitter.com and search for something like #gbl (games-based learning). This search retrieves tweets from people all over the planet talking about games-based learning who are sharing articles, models, resources, and questions.

Most of the hashtags listed are well established. While #medialiteracy is the emerging hashtag for all things media and education, we'd like to suggest #mediaed as a shorter and more inclusive alternative. When using a medium like Twitter where communication can be only 140 characters long, the difference between typing *literacy* and *ed* is a large one. We don't know that our little book will inspire a trend toward #mediaed, but we think it is worth a try.

Adding to hashtag suggestions, Ryan's @_mindblue_ Twitter account contains curated lists of "people to follow" related to every medium at the account's list page (twitter.com/_mindblue_/lists). These lists are built around the resources in this chapter and are constantly being updated. We'll also try to utilize #mcpop as the tag for everything related to the book.

Third, the resources listed are very diverse. We tried in each section to include texts within a category, information about the way texts are created, some exemplary models, resources that deal with the history and culture of the type of text, and information about their use in the K–12 classroom. When possible, we're including works that address academic rationales for the use of each text type.

Many of the suggested texts will be great for classroom use, but other texts are more for you as the teacher or for students who really want to dig deep into the creation of a specific medium. As you explore the resources you will be able to make those judgments.

If you recall, in Chapter 2 we presented a series of big guiding questions. Question number 3 was, "Is this text appropriate for your students developmentally and culturally?" We can't stress enough that you must *always preview texts in their entirety*. Don't put yourself in a position where you will be surprised. As long as you make mindful choices around texts and use the LEOs as artifacts/data that demonstrate student learning, you will be able to make your curriculum pop while developing student literacies.

Finally, we want to highlight that the Cultural Artifacts category presently acts as a catchall for very diverse texts, including objects and spaces. We hope, over time, to refine this category based on feedback from readers like you.

Basic Resources

These resources are helpful across many disciplines:

○ *American Masters* is a PBS television series that has been producing biographies of American cultural luminaries since 1986. Many musicians working in every genre have been profiled on the show. You can search the series for music profiles (pbs.org/wnet/americanmasters /category/episodes/by-topic) and educator resources (pbs.org/wnet /americanmasters/category/for-educators).

○ *Hot: One World, One Climate* by Carolyn Harris, Pushker Kharecha, and Ryan Goble (2013). This curriculum and simulation is a collaborative effort among secondary teachers, educational experts, and journalists with faculty and staff from the NASA Goddard Institute for Space Studies (GISS) and the Columbia University Earth Institute. This interdisciplinary curriculum is loaded with a wide range of texts to explore some of the largest challenges facing our planet. Videos and units can be accessed at www.giss.nasa.gov/edu/ccic/nodes/node24.html.

○ Making Curriculum Pop (mcpopmb.ning.com)—otherwise known as MC POP—is a social network we created and maintain for thousands of teachers from all over the globe. The site is free, and you can sign in using a Facebook or Gmail ID. When you enter the site, you'll see teachers sharing and discussing better practices and the use of popular cultures in the classroom. Ryan usually tweets these resources at @_mindblue_, so consider following him there as well. We have posted many resources in the book as hyperlinked webpages at MC POP. We hope that you will join us there and continue the discussion by adding your ideas in the groups that interest you, including one dedicated to this book (mcpopmb.ning.com/group/mcpopdlaca).

○ *Made Here* (madehereproject.org) is a documentary series that explores the lives and issues of performing artists living in New York City. It is a great peek behind the scenes of the art, dance, music, and theater worlds.

○ *Makers* on PBS boasts "the largest video collection of women's stories" (makers.com); it is also responsible for the documentary *MAKERS: Women Who Made America,* which captures the story of the modern American women's movement.

○ The Media Literacy Clearinghouse (frankwbaker.com) is loaded with resources and lesson plans for the use of nonprint texts. In 2012, Frank Baker also published the book *Media Literacy in the K–12 Classroom*, a practical starting point for those interested in learning about traditional media literacy practices.

○ The Media Education Lab (mediaeducationlab.com) at the University of Rhode Island's Harrington School of Communication and Media specializes in training teachers around media education and offers a wide range of interactive resources for students and teachers. One of the most informative things at their website is their work with educators and politicians around copyright issues in the classroom, as they apply to media.

○ The *New York Times* Learning Network (learning.blogs.nytimes.com) is one of the most comprehensive websites available for teachers interested in integrating excellent journalism practices in multiple texts with any discipline. Be sure to join their mailing list to receive daily lesson plans and other resources during the school year.

○ *A People's Curriculum for the Earth: Teaching Climate Change and the Environmental Crisis* (2014), edited by Bill Bigelow. This essential anthology from Rethinking Schools explores many texts, from food and water systems to the commodification of nature to plastics as an energy source. Loaded with diverse texts (and ideas for exploring them in the classroom), this book will work in any discipline.

○ Project Look Sharp (ithaca.edu/looksharp) at Ithaca College is an organization dedicated to training K–college teachers on the teaching of media texts across the curriculum. In addition to training programs for teachers, they offer wonderful downloadable curriculum kits and lesson plans on topics like "The Causes of the American Revolution," "Media Construction of Endangered Species," and "Media Constructions of Martin Luther King."

○ The Science and Entertainment Exchange (scienceandentertainment exchange.org) is a Los Angeles–based program of the National Academy of Science designed to connect scientists with media producers. While they are not creating lessons per se, all of their features, projects, and videos are loaded with ideas to connect popular culture and science in a wide variety of high-interest texts.

○ *Rethinking Popular Culture and Media* (2011), edited by Elizabeth Marshall and Özlem Sensoy, is a must-have anthology of articles and ideas from *Rethinking Schools* magazine (rethinkingschools.org). Many of the articles are narratives from teachers who use some aspect of popular culture and media in their classrooms. Other articles take on large topics like the relationship between corporations and schooling.

○ TED and TED-ED (ted.com & ed.ted.com) collect the popular TED Talks series of five- to twenty-minute video talks and animations about "ideas worth sharing." Both sites are easily browsable by topic, theme, or disciplinary keywords.

Advertising

Billboards, Promotions, Print, TV, and Online
Mindblue Twitter List: twitter.com/_mindblue_/lists/mcpop-advertising1
Twitter Hashtags: #advertisting, #ad, #aded

Advertising texts are designed to sell a product, idea, or even a person (e.g., in political campaigns). Unless you live in a very remote area, you're likely to be bombarded by ads. This can be as obvious as a billboard or TV commercial or as subtle as putting Reese's Pieces in a film like *E.T.* These texts want to persuade their audience to act in a certain way. To do this they use sophisticated techniques to establish trust and credibility.

Advertising is usually targeted at specific demographics. In the past, the demographic categories were large, e.g., women ages eighteen to thirty-five. But the digital age is leading toward focusing on the demographic of one person. Now many ads are targeted to respond to an individual's Internet browsing history.

Some Useful LEOs

Archaeologist, Archivist, Body Linguist, Connector, Data Analyst, Demographer, Designer, Fact Checker, Framer, Lawyer, Producer, Sensor, Summarizer, Sound Mixer (for audio/video ads), Wonderer, Worldviewer

Starting Points

BOOKS

○ *Branded: The Buying & Selling of Teenagers* (2004) by Alissa Quart explicates the way brands exploit adolescents.

○ *Confessions of an Advertising Man* (2012) by David Ogilvy. This British-born adman founded Ogilvy & Mather's in 1948 in New York City. Considered by many to be the original "Mad Man," Ogilvy recounts his story and groundbreaking advertising strategies in this seminal memoir.

○ *No Logo* (2009) by Naomi Klein. In this text Klein explores the ubiquity of brand imagery and the problematic practices of international corporations.

○ *Made You Look: How Advertising Works and Why You Should Know About It* (2003) by Shari Graydon and Warren Clark. This text, written for middle school/junior high students, explores common advertising techniques and breaks down ad campaigns with the goal of helping young people be more critical consumers.

○ *Twenty Ads That Shook the World: The Century's Most Groundbreaking Advertising and How It Changed Us All* (2000) by James B. Twitchell. This book explores the advertising campaigns and their creators that

Twitchell feels have had the greatest impact on 20th century history and culture.

○ *Political Campaigns and Political Advertising: A Media Literacy Guide* (2009) by Frank W. Baker. This teacher-friendly guide is loaded with "behind the scenes" case studies. Baker illuminates ways that teachers can explore these persuasive messages through a media literacy framework.

WEBSITES

○ Adbusters (adbusters.org) is a nonprofit, Vancouver-based online and print magazine. Their artwork inspired the Occupy Wall Street movement and their interdisciplinary approach is "concerned about the impact of commercial forces on personal and cultural spaces."

○ Admongo (admongo.gov) is a game and curriculum developed by the Federal Trade Commission (FTC) and Scholastic. The interface is designed to develop tweens' (ages eight to twelve) advertising literacy.

○ "The Deconstruction Gallery" (medialiteracyproject.org/deconstructions) by the Media Literacy Project breaks down advertisements into their rhetorical parts.

○ "Don't Buy It: Get Media Smart" (pbskids.org/dontbuyit) is a PBS Kids webpage designed to help third through fifth graders question, analyze, interpret, and evaluate media messages. Many of the activities there are easily scaled up for secondary students.

○ Advertising Age (adage.com) and AdWeek (adweek.com) are trade publications for the advertising industry. Teachers in many disciplines will find these sites to be rich in short texts that illuminate techniques, personalities, and budgets behind familiar brands.

○ The "Advertising Group" (mcpopmb.ning.com/group/advertising) at Making Curriculum Pop is a social network forum for teachers to share questions and resources about integrating advertising into the classroom.

○ The *New York Times* Learning Network Advertising Lesson Plans (learning.blogs.nytimes.com/category/lesson-plans/text-studies /advertising) uses a wide range of *Times* content. Print articles are emphasized, but they also explore images, video, and infographics and supply a wide range of graphic organizers for educators to explore current advertising stories while connecting teachers with additional archive content.

○ *This American Life,* Episode 133: Sales (thisamericanlife.org/radio-archives/episode/133/sales). *This American Life* is a radio show produced by Public Radio International and aired on public radio stations all over the country. This hour-long episode is broken into four short acts that explore America's talent for the art of selling.

FILMS

○ *Art and Copy: Inside Advertising's Creative Revolution* (2010) directed by Doug Pray introduces viewers to some of the creative ideas behind the most memorable advertisements of our time.

○ *Killing Us Softly 4: Advertising's Image of Women* (2010) directed by Sut Jhally (available at mediaed.org) is a forty-five-minute presentation by internationally recognized women's advocate Jean Kilbourne on how advertising affects perceptions of women in our society.

○ *Frontline*, "The Merchants of Cool" (2001), directed by Barak Goodman. Media critic Douglas Rushkoff looks at corporate America's obsession with marketing and selling products to teenage consumers in this episode of the long-running TV show.

○ *Frontline*, "The Persuaders" (2005), directed by Barak Goodman and Rachel Dretzin. This episode uncovers the often-surprising ways advertising and public relations firms influence our daily lives and habits.

○ *The Greatest Movie Ever Sold* (2011) by Morgan Spurlock is a journey into the world of film and TV product placement.

○ *POPaganda: The Art and Subversion of Ron English* (2004) directed by Pedro Carvajal is a short film (available on YouTube) that explores the mixed-text art of English's "culture jamming." Like graffiti artists, English will illegally take over public spaces (usually billboards) and remix the ads of large corporations with his own, often comic, anti-consumerist critiques.

○ *A Walk Through the 20th Century with Bill Moyers*, "The 30-Second President" (1984), directed by Martin Koughan. This episode explores presidential campaign ads from Kennedy v. Nixon through the Reagan era and is filled with archival footage and interviews with candidates and their ad makers. Many academic libraries have this film; it is also available for purchase through the Films for Humanities and Science site (ffh.films.com).

In humanities classes it is exciting to find old print ads for students to explore using LEOs. Many books collect vintage ads, but you can also explore websites like the Vintage Ad Browser (vintageadbrowser.com) or the Advertising Archives (advertisingarchives.co.uk) for images. Also, you might enjoy using LEOs to explore presidential campaign ads. Ease History (goo.gl/1Drpcq) has a comprehensive database of campaign videos searchable by year.

In STEM classes we look at how scientific or mathematical claims are made by advertisements. Advertising is notorious for making scientific claims and selectively presenting research. Assessing how ads use and abuse math and scientific research is an excellent use of LEOs. A great starting point for those interested in reading case studies about these things is *Innumeracy: Mathematical Illiteracy and Its Consequences* (2001) by John Allen Paulos.

Audio

Nonmusic Radio and Podcasts

Mindblue Twitter List: twitter.com/_mindblue_/lists/mcpop-audio1
Twitter Hashtags: #audioed, #npr, #podcasting, #radio

Audio text is sound, especially sound which is recorded, transmitted, or reproduced. Audio also relates to the broadcasting or reception of sound. While music certainly is an audio text, our focus for this category is narrative audio, which was once the domain of radio, but now also includes podcasts and audio documentaries. Talk radio in all its forms (including digital) is excellent material for classroom study.

Some Useful LEOs

Archaeologist, Archivist, Demographer, Fact Checker, Framer, Highlighter, Performer, Sensor, Set Designer, Sociologist, Sound Mixer, Time Catcher, Timeliner, Visualizer, Wonderer

Starting Points

BOOKS

○ *Drop That Knowledge: Youth Radio Stories* (2010) by Lisa Soep and Vivian Chavez. Underserved students flock to the Peabody Award–winning Youth Radio workshops based in Oakland, California. This book takes readers inside this organization, interweaving personal narratives of participating students.

○ *Hello, Everybody! The Dawn of American Radio* (2008) by Anthony Rudel traces the birth of American radio from a motley crew of eccentrics and visionaries to the prominent text in mid-20th-century America.

○ *Podcasting at School* (2008) by Kristin Fontichiaro introduces the podcasting medium by dispelling myths about Web 2.0 in the classroom and continues by defining the medium and giving clear instructions and ideas for teachers hoping to podcast in their own classrooms.

○ *Radio: An Illustrated Guide* (1999) by Jessica Abel and Ira Glass is a short graphic novel that takes listeners and aspiring radio producers into the process of creating the innovative (and award-winning) public radio show *This American Life*.

○ *Theatre of the Mind: Writing and Producing Radio Dramas in the Classroom* (2004) by Don Kisner is a helpful manual written by a classroom teacher for those interested in creating radio dramas in the classroom.

WEBSITES

○ *This American Life* (thisamericanlife.org) also has an educator's site (thisamericanlife.org/education) that sorts episodes by disciplines and grade level. Ryan also wrote two blogs at the *School Library Journal's* "Connect the Pop" blog about using *This American Life* in the classroom—see "Uncommon Literacies: Teaching 'This American Life' (1)" (goo.gl/he1ET) and "Uncommon Literacies: Teaching 'This American Life' (2)" (goo.gl/PNk7t0).

○ *Backstory with the American History Guys* on NPR (backstoryradio.org) brings historians together to discuss and reexamine historical events, ideas, and themes.

○ The Chicago Historical Society collects and maintains "historical voice galleries," including the work of the famous oral historian Studs Terkel (historicalvoices.org/sitemap.php). The society is also working in partnership with the Library of Congress to digitize all of Terkel's interviews with famous 20th-century Americans. See Terkel's website (studsterkelcentenary.wordpress.com/resources) for updates on his oral histories and related resources.

o   Dan Carlin's Hardcore History podcast (dancarlin.com/hardcore-history-series) weaves historical storylines together into edge-of-your-seat narratives.

o   Generic Radio Workshop is a group of radio artists who recreate performances of vintage radio plays in and around Texas. Their site maintains a Vintage Radio Script Library (genericradio.com/library.php) that includes full scripts of many famous shows from the era.

o   iTunes' Podcast Directory (apple.com/itunes/podcasts) allows you to search for podcasts on virtually any subject, including courses and programs from major academic institutions.

o   The Mercury Theatre on the Air (mercurytheatre.info) is a website maintained by an individual working on archiving all of Orson Welles's radio theater troupe's radio shows to stream or download online.

o   *The Moth* is a forum for live storytelling events (themoth.org) shared online and on NPR. This eclectic collection of narratives includes many that can easily be connected to classroom curricula. Click on the "support" tab at the website to read about the MOTHshop Community Education Program.

o   The Museum of Broadcast Communications (museum.tv) in Chicago also hosts the Radio Hall of Fame (radiohof.org). This institution collects, preserves, and presents historic and contemporary radio and television content. In addition to their extensive archives, their education department curates materials and develops teaching resources for classroom use.

o   The *New York Times* Learning Network Audio and Radio lesson plans (learning.blogs.nytimes.com/category/lesson-plans/text-studies/audio-and-radio) use a wide range of *Times* content. Print articles are emphasized, but they also explore images, video, and infographics and supply a wide range of graphic organizers for educators to explore stories related to audio and radio while connecting teachers with additional archive content.

o   National Public Radio's (NPR) "Driveway Moments" (npr.org/series/700000/driveway-moments). A "driveway moment" is a radio story that is so compelling that you need to sit in your driveway to hear the end of the story. This site collects these from all of NPR's programming in the early 2000s.

○ The Paley Center for Media (paleycenter.org) has locations in New York City and Los Angeles and was originally called the Museum of Television and Radio but was renamed in 2007 to reflect a wider range of media. Both locations have searchable archives and educational departments that work with K–college teachers and students at every level.

○ *A Prairie Home Companion with Garrison Keillor* (prairiehome.org) keeps the tradition of radio variety shows alive. With a mix of music, fiction, and nonfiction, Keillor explores 21st-century life through the lens of classic radio.

○ *Radiolab* is a National Public Radio show and podcast that connects stories, sounds, and science (radiolab.org). As explained at the show's website, it is a "show about curiosity, where sound illuminates ideas, and the boundaries blur between science, philosophy, and human experience."

○ Radio Spirits (radiospirits.com) has digitized classic old-time radio programs. Their catalog emphasizes American radio programs from the 1930s to the 1960s in every genre.

○ The website Slate's *Working* podcast (slate.com/articles/podcasts /working.html) explores how all kinds of people do their jobs.

○ Story Corps (storycorps.org) is modeled on the WPA (Works Progress Administration) oral history programs of the 1930s. By setting up booths all over the country, Story Corps collects 21st-century oral histories from a wide range of people. Recently, they have started animating some of the more compelling stories. Story Corps founder Dave Isay's TED Talk "Everyone Around You Has a Story the World Needs to Hear" nicely introduces the project and its vision (bit.ly/1FA9d6s).

○ Youth Radio (youthradio.org) is a Peabody Award–winning educational organization that develops and shares youth-produced journalism created by students in Oakland, California; Washington, D.C.; Atlanta, Georgia; and Los Angeles, California. Many of their productions are featured on NPR.

FILMS

○ *Empire of the Air: The Men Who Made Radio* (2004) directed by Ken Burns is a riveting documentary about three dramatically different Americans who made radio big business in the early 20th-century.

○ "Ira Glass on Storytelling," a four-part interview (2009) by Current TV, is available on YouTube. In these clips, Glass, host of *This American Life,* explains how to build story for radio.

- PBS's *American Masters,* "Garrison Keillor: The Man on the Radio in Red Shoes" (2009), directed by Peter Rosen, is an engaging biography of radio star Garrison Keillor. This can be coupled with the film *A Prairie Home Companion* (2006) directed by Robert Altman.

- *This American Life: Behind the Scenes* (2009) by *This American Life* is available at store.thisamericanlife.org. This interview with the entire TAL production staff explains how a weekly radio show goes from idea to production.

- *Radio Days* (1987) directed by Woody Allen is a coming-of-age film paralleling the life of a young Brooklyn teen with the backstage drama of radio's biggest stars in the 1930s.

- *Back of the Mike* (1938) by Jam Handy Organization for the Chevrolet Motor Company is a wonderful short film about how sound effects are produced for radio; it can be found on YouTube.

In humanities classes it is easy to search a show like *This American Life* for a theme related to whatever content you are interested in exploring. Most of the *This American Life* episodes are broken into short acts that are excellent for teaching literacy concepts. Some standout episodes for social studies teachers include "Man vs. History," "Wrong Side of History," and "Pinned by History," as they can be used with any historical period one is studying.

In STEM classes, NPR's *Radiolab* (radiolab.org), *Science Friday* (sciencefriday.com), and *The Math Guy Radio Archive* from *Weekend Edition* (stanford.edu/~kdevlin/MathGuy.html) present stunning STEM narratives for LEO-based exploration.

Comics

Graphic Novels and Sequential Art

Mindblue Twitter List: twitter.com/_mindblue_/lists/mcpop-comics1
Twitter Hashtags: #arted, #artsed, #comicsed, #edcomics

Comics also encompass graphic novels and/or sequential art. Generally speaking, a comic is the shorter three- or four-panel daily strip that became popular in newspapers. This format evolved into comic books. The graphic novel is often perceived as a more sophisticated form of sequential art that explores ideas in various genres, at times with the depth of great literature. Fiction and nonfiction graphic novels are used more and more often in the K–12 classroom.

Some Useful LEOs

Blogger, Body Linguist, Cartoonist, Casting Director, Dialogue Master, Fashion Critic, Gamer, Genre Guru, Highlighter, Hypothesizer, Imagery Hunter, Mood Catcher, Plot Master, Producer, Summarizer, Wonderer, Wordsmith, Worldviewer

Starting Points

BOOKS

○ *Building Literacy Connections with Graphic Novels: Page by Page, Panel by Panel* (2007) edited by James Bucky Carter. This volume showcases an impressive range of ideas on how educators can link traditional texts with graphic novels in the classroom.

○ *Drawing Words and Writing Pictures: Making Comics: Manga, Graphic Novels, and Beyond* (2008) by Jessica Abel and Matt Madden. Abel and Madden are a husband-and-wife team known equally for their artwork and educational initiatives. This is an excellent primer for aspiring comics creators.

○ *Faster Than a Speeding Bullet: The Rise of the Graphic Novel* (2004) by Stephen Weiner is an excellent book for teachers looking for an understanding of the evolution of comics into today's popular graphic novels.

○ *The Graphic Novel Classroom: POWerful Teaching and Learning with Images* (2011) by Maureen M. Bakis. This book presents a series of user-friendly lessons built around graphic novels and a wide range of literacy and critical thinking skills.

○ *Teaching Graphic Novels: Practical Strategies for the Secondary ELA Classroom* (2009) and *Teaching Early Reader Comics and Graphic Novels* (2011) by Katie Monnin. These texts offer teachers a rationale for using graphic novels in the classroom as stand-alone curriculum and as bridges to traditional curriculum. Loaded with graphic organizers and resource suggestions, these are essential books for those interested in making their practice "graphic."

○ *The TOON Treasury of Classic Children's Comics* (2009) edited by Françoise Mouly and Art Spiegelman. While written for emerging readers, this anthology of short, familiar stories is an excellent resource for teachers interested in short, artistically complex comics for student exploration.

○ *Understanding Comics: The Invisible Art* (2000) and *Making Comics: Storytelling Secrets of Comics, Manga and Graphic Novels* (2006) by Scott McCloud. The former book is a canonical exploration of the language, history, and theory behind comics, and the latter emphasizes the "how to's" of a comic's creation.

○ *Unflattening* (2015) by Nick Sousanis is based on the first comic book dissertation. This experiment in visual thinking is an inquiry into the ways we construct knowledge through words and image.

WEBSITES

○ The Comic Book Project (comicbookproject.org) is an international non-profit organization that works with educational organizations serving K–12 students to create comics for publication.

○ The Comics Workshop (marekbennett.com/comicsworkshop) is a site about Marek Bennett's comic education projects. The site includes videos, teacher resources, samples of student work, and links to Bennett's personal comics about teaching the art form to young people all over the world.

○ The Drawing Words and Writing Pictures Blog (dw-wp.com) is the comics education site maintained by author-artists and teachers Jessica Abel and Matt Madden. The site has features that speak to the novice artist as well as the seasoned professional.

○ EN/SANE (English Education and Sequential Art Narratives in Education) World Blog (ensaneworld.blogspot.com) by James Bucky Carter explores academic, commercial, and pedagogical issues surrounding the use of comics in the classroom.

○ The "Graphic Novel Group" at Making Curriculum Pop (mcpopmb.ning .com/group/graphicnovelscomics) is perhaps the most vibrant of the social networks at the site. This forum counts many top comic artists and educators as members. For that reason it is an excellent place to find resources and ask questions about integrating comics into the classroom.

○ *The Graphic Novel Reporter* (graphicnovelreporter.com) is an online magazine for teachers and librarians interested in reviews of the latest graphic novels, as well as interviews with their creators.

- Graphic Novel Resources Blog (graphicnovelresources.blogspot.com) is a site maintained by University of Tennessee education professor Stergios Botzakis where he shares weekly reviews of graphic novels for young adults across every discipline.

- Make Beliefs Comix (makebeliefscomix.com) is an educational comics creator where kids can create their own comics using stock artwork. Additionally, the site's creator, Bill Zimmerman, maintains a rich library of printable comics built around themes, allowing the students to add to the frames and create dialogue.

- Toon Books (toon-books.com) publishes comics for emerging readers using top-notch comic artists. This publishing house was created by *New Yorker* cover editor Françoise Mouly and is designed to engage early readers.

- The Toonseum (toonseum.org) in Pittsburgh, Pennsylvania, is a small museum dedicated to the comic and cartoon arts.

FILMS

Before listing some existing films—mostly nonfiction—about comics and their creators, it is worth noting that contemporary graphic novelists are a diverse bunch and most have a strong Web presence. If you are interested in a particular author/artist, do a search at places like YouTube.com and NPR to see if any short documentaries or interviews are available.

- PBS's *American Masters,* "Good Ol' Charles Schulz" (2007), directed by David Van Taylor. This biography uses Schulz's archives and interviews with his friends and collaborators to appreciate his life and the fifty-year run of his *Peanuts* comic strips.

- *The Cartoonist: Jeff Smith, BONE and the Changing Face of Comics* (2009) directed by Ken Mills. This documentary tells the story of Smith's creation of the critical and commercial smash *BONE.*

- *Comic Book Confidential* (1988) directed by Ron Mann. This documentary explores the history of the comics medium from the 1930s—including the censorship of comics—through their pinnacle in the 1980s. The documentary features interviews with many top comics artists and writers.

- *Comic-Con Episode IV: A Fan's Hope* (2012) directed by Morgan Spurlock. Spurlock, a documentary filmmaker known for his documentary *Supersize Me,* talks with comics-loving celebrities and superfans at San Diego's world-renowned Comic-Con convention.

○ *Will Eisner: Profession—Cartoonist* (1999) directed by Marisa Furtado de Oliveira and Paulo Serran. This documentary explores the career of pioneering cartoonist Will Eisner, who was known for creating the Spirit in the 1940s and for groundbreaking graphic novels that redefined the artistic measures of the medium. The third part of the film captures Eisner giving a master class on his creative process.

In humanities classes graphic novels are widely becoming an essential part of secondary curricula across the globe. A staggering selection of historical graphic novels and comics has been published in the last ten years. To start, Larry Gonick's The Cartoon History of series; the graphic adaptation of Howard Zinn's *A People's History of the American Empire* (2008); Hill and Wang's graphic novel collection including biographies of Malcolm X, J. Edgar Hoover, Anne Frank, Ronald Reagan, and Leon Trotsky; as well as the efforts of major textbook companies like McGraw-Hill/Jamestown Education's World History Ink series (glencoe.com/gln/jamestown/world_history_ink.html) are tremendous resources.

In STEM classes, many authors and publishers are taking sequential-art approaches to math, science, and technology. Three favorites include Jim Ottaviani's publications from G. T. Labs (gt-labs.com), Jay Hosler's comics about biology and Darwin (jayhosler.com/cartoonist.html), and the amazing illustrative posters on biotechnology from the South African Department of Science and Technology (goo.gl/nqnbR).

Cultural Artifacts

Architecture, Body Art, Cars, Dance, Ecosystems, Fashion, Food, Industrial Design, Landscape, Toys

Mindblue Twitter List: twitter.com/_mindblue_/lists/mcpop-cultural-artifacts

Twitter Hashtags: #architects, #arted, #artsed, #cars, #climatechange, #foodlit, #fooded, #dance, #danceed, #design, #eco, #fashion, #green, #landscape, #toys, #mediaed, #medialiteracy, #museumed

Obviously, all texts can be considered cultural artifacts. As such, this section is designed to catch a wide range of objects worthy of study in mediums that are not traditionally regarded as texts. Some artifacts might be of great cultural significance, such as the Taj Mahal or the design of Central Park in New York City. Other objects might not be considered high culture, such as a collection of postcards, shoes, body art, movie posters, magazines, a bowling alley, or the toys at a local store. Other items occupy a wide range of cultural spaces, such as cars: these are collected, are showcased in museums, and are exciting to explore from a cultural, technological, and artistic point of view. They tell the story of a particular time period.

In many situations you will be looking at still images of things in magazines, books, posters, museums, or on the Internet. That said, we hope you will create opportunities for students to explore public spaces when possible.

Some Useful LEOs

Archaeologist, Archivist, Blogger, Designer, Geographer, Hypothesizer, Imagery Hunter, Intuitor, Mood Catcher, Poet, Predictor, Producer, Sensor, Summarizer, Tech Specialist, Wonderer, Worldviewer

Starting Points

BOOKS

○ *American Eden: From Monticello to Central Park to Our Backyards: What Our Gardens Tell Us About Who We Are* (2011) by Wade Graham. This book focuses on a collection of photos and illustrations coupled with an analysis of America's most significant gardens and their creators.

○ *The Beatles in 100 Objects* (2013) by Brian Southall explores the Fab Four through their most famous things.

○ *Books That Cook: The Making of a Literary Meal* (2014) edited by Jennifer Cognard-Black and Melissa Goldthwaite uses the cookbook format to collect American literature written on the theme of food.

○ *Castle* (1977), *Cathedral* (1973), *Pyramid* (1975), *Great Moments in Architecture* (1978), or any architecture book by David Macaulay. Every one of Macaulay's books is powerful because he creates a fictional architectural story of, say, a generic castle from his research on the building of many castles. In this way readers and viewers (many of these books were made into PBS specials) are transported into a culture through architecture.

- *A Curious History of Food and Drink* (2014) by Ian Crofton explores history through short anecdotes about the things we eat and drink.

- *Earth in Mind: On Education, Environment, and the Human Prospect* (2004) by David W. Orr is a collection of essays about educating for a sustainable planet.

- *Ecoliterate: How Educators Are Cultivating Emotional, Social, and Ecological Intelligence* (2012) by Daniel Goleman, Lisa Bennett, and Zenobia Barlow discusses how teachers and their students can read and write our ecosystems.

- *An Edible History of Humanity* (2011) and *The History of the World in Six Glasses* (2006) by Tom Standage. These two books use food and beverages to share the connections between humanity's most vital needs and their links to historical events and technological innovations. Pulling excerpts from these texts is a powerful way to start the discussion about this topic.

- *Humans of New York* (2013) and *Little Humans* (2014) by Brandon Stanton are based on his popular photography blog and collect curious and captivating portraits of people and their worlds.

- *Learning the Landscape: Inquiry-Based Activities for Comprehending and Composing* (1996) by Fran Claggett, Louann Reid, and Ruth Vinz is written for humanities students and teachers interested in exploring "our relationships to our surroundings, neighborhoods, and the ecological system."

- *Lives of the Trees: An Uncommon History* (2010) by Diana Wells.

- *Material World: A Global Family Portrait* (1995), *Hungry Planet: What the World Eats* (2007), and *What I Eat: Around the World in 80 Diets* (2010) are all by photographer Peter Menzel. His work is focused on capturing individuals and families all over the world with the food that they eat. The Social Studies School Service (socialstudies.com) has bundled the *Material World* book with a series of PowerPoint presentations and posters designed for classroom use.

- *The Meaning of Trees: Botany, History, Healing, Lore* (2005) by Fred Hageneder.

- *A Perfect Red: Empire, Espionage, and the Quest for the Color of Desire* (2006) by Amy Butler Greenfield. This text explores how a cultural object—a legendary red dye that Spanish conquistadors brought back to Europe—influenced the life and times of three centuries of Europeans.

- *Reading the Landscape of America* (1999) by May Theilgaard Watts is a natural history classic from 1975 that teaches readers how to "read" their surroundings.

- *The Reason for Flowers: Their History, Culture, and Biology, and How They Change Our Lives* (2015) by Stephen Buchmann is a cultural history of humans' relationship to flowers.

- *Seeing Trees: Discover the Extraordinary Secrets of Everyday Trees* (2011) by Nancy R. Hugo and Robert Llewellyn.

- *Seven Flowers: And How They Shaped Our World* (2015) by Jennifer Potter. Learn how the lotus, the lily, the sunflower, the opium poppy, the rose, the tulip, and the orchid impact our lives in surprising ways.

- *Shakespeare's Restless World: A Portrait of an Era in Twenty Objects* (2013) by Neil MacGregor.

- *The Smithsonian's History of America in 101 Objects* (2013) by Richard Kurin.

- *The Tree: A Natural History of What Trees Are, How They Live, and Why They Matter* (2007) by Colin Tudge.

- *An Uncommon History of Common Courtesy: How Manners Shaped the World* (2011) by Bethanne Patrick.

- *An Uncommon History of Common Things* (2009) by Bethanne Patrick and John Thompson.

- *Why Design? Projects from the National Building Museum* (1995) by Anna Slafer and Kevin Cahill. Although this book is out of print, used copies are available. It is an excellent primer for teachers who want to explore "design thinking" in their classrooms.

MAGAZINES/JOURNALS

- *Architectural Digest* (architecturaldigest.com) is an excellent place to explore the most fascinating dwellings on the planet.

- *Audubon Magazine* (audubonmagazine.org) explores the relationship of birds to our natural environments.

- *Earth Island Journal* (earthisland.org/journal) covers a wide range of environmental issues as they relate to place, persons, and species. It is published by David Brower's nonprofit Earth Island Institute.

o *Ecotone* (ecotonejournal.com) is the University of North Carolina–
Wilmington's award-winning literary magazine that "brings together
the literary and the scientific, the personal and the biological, the urban
and the rural" as they relate to place.

o Fashion magazines: there are likely too many of these to list, but *W*
(wmagazine.com), *Interview* (interviewmagazine.com), and *InStyle*
(instyle.com) are just some you might use as classroom texts.

o *National Geographic* (nationalgeographic.com) is still one of the greatest
magazines for visualizing the places, spaces, and objects of the diverse
inhabitants of our world.

o *OnEarth* (onearth.org), the magazine of the National Resources Defense
Council, reads like an environmental version of *Entertainment Weekly*.

o *Orion Magazine* (orionmagazine.org) "brings ideas, writers, photogra-
phers, and artists together, focused on nature, the environment, and
culture, addressing environmental and societal issues."

o *Smithsonian Magazine* (smithsonianmag.com) shares narratives related
to objects and exhibits related to the Smithsonian family of museums.

WEBSITES

In addition to the following resources, be sure to also explore the museums
listed in the visual arts section.

o *99% Invisible* (99percentinvisible.org) is a radio show "about the built
world, about things manufactured by humans."

o 350.org (350.org) is an organization dedicated to addressing one of the
most pressing issues of our time: climate change. What makes 350.org
relevant for those looking for cultural texts is that they use novel methods to make this invisible issue visible, including EARTH (earth.350.org),
the world's first global satellite art project.

o The Artist Project (artistproject.metmuseum.org) is a Web series produced by the Metropolitan Museum of Art where artists share their
thoughts on specific works in the museum's collection.

o BBC Radio 4's *A History of the World in 100 Objects* podcasts (bbc.co.uk
/podcasts/series/ahow) showcase over two million years of human
invention and innovation. The series is curated by Neil MacGregor,
director of the British Museum. MacGregor also authored a book based
on the series with the same title (2011).

o The Center for Ecoliteracy (ecoliteracy.org) is a public foundation dedicated to education for sustainable living.

- "Hands On" by the Museums Galleries Scotland is "a step-by-step guide to learning with museum objects and paintings" (museumsgalleries scotland.org.uk/research-and-resources/resources/learning-and-access /formal-learning-and-museums/what-is-hands-on).

- The Henry Ford Museum in Dearborn, Michigan (thehenryford.org /education), is a ninety-acre indoor and outdoor history museum exploring the American Experience. The collection highlights famous homes, machinery, and Americana. Collection highlights include things like the Wright Brothers' bicycle shop, Rosa Parks's bus, and Abraham Lincoln's chair from the Ford Theatre.

- *The Meaning of Food* (2004) directed by Karin Williams is a PBS special that explores the relationships between life, family, culture, and food. See related lesson plans at pbs.org/opb/meaningoffood/classroom.

- The Museum of Arts and Design in New York City (madmuseum.org) is dedicated to the preservation, study, and display of contemporary hand-made objects in a wide range of texts.

- Museum of Latin American Art (molaa.org) in Long Beach, California, maintains a website with educator resources on their exhibitions.

- The Museum of Mathematics (MOMATH) in New York City (momath .org) opened its doors—appropriately—on 12/12/12. This museum shares math-themed artifacts through their Facebook page; their education department is one to watch as the museum evolves.

- The National Building Museum (nbm.org) in Washington, D.C., tells the "stories of architecture, engineering, and design." Click on their schools/educator tab to explore their workshops and curriculum kits.

- The National Museum of African American History and Culture (nmaahc.si.edu) is one of the newest Smithsonian Museums in Washington, D.C. In addition to their educator resources, they offer a classroom video conferencing series called "The Lives of Objects."

- The National Museum of the American Indian in Washington, D.C. (nmai.si.edu) maintains an extensive collection of objects and art at their website.

- The National Museum of American History's "The Object of History" learning guide (objectofhistory.org) is a great source for cultural objects.

- The *New York Times* Learning Network fashion (learning.blogs.nytimes .com/tag/fashion) and popular culture (learning.blogs.nytimes.com /category/lesson-plans/text-studies/popular-culture) lesson plans use a wide range of *Times* content. Print articles are emphasized, but they also explore images, video, and infographics and supply a wide range of graphic organizers for educators to explore stories related to popular culture and fashion while connecting teachers with additional archival content.

○ The *New York Times* "History of New York in 50 Objects" (nytimes.com /interactive/2012/09/02/nyregion/a-history-of-new-york-in-50-objects .html).

○ Schomburg Center for Research in Black Culture (nypl.org/locations /schomburg) is a branch of the New York Public Library that collects, preserves, and provides access to the study of the cultures of people of African descent. The "Digital Schomburg" tab features online exhibitions including an Images and Illustration collection.

○ The Smithsonian Museum Education Department (smithsonian education.org/educators) in Washington, D.C., has a vast collection of lesson plans divided into the four major categories of "Art and Design," "Science and Technology," "History and Culture," and "Language Arts." Educators can search by grade, subject, and topic. See also the Smithsonian National Museum of American History's "Engaging Students with Primary Sources" curriculum at (historyexplorer.si.edu /teacher).

○ The SOAS Food Studies Centre at the University of London "is an inter-disciplinary centre dedicated to the study of the political, economic, and cultural dimensions of food, historically and in the contemporary moment, from production, to exchange, to preparation, to consumption" (www.soas.ac.uk/foodstudies).

○ Teaching and Learning Resources from the Federal Registry for Educational Excellence (free.ed.gov) collects animations, primary documents, photos, and videos from a wide range of government organizations and designs lesson plans around select texts. This site is also searchable by topic, discipline, and grade level.

○ Time Out New York's (TONY) entertaining "Public Eye" section (timeoutnewyork.com/publiceye) uses everyday fashion as a window into the cultures of New York City.

○ The United States National Archives maintains a website for teachers called Docs Teach (docsteach.org) built around helping teachers use primary source documents (including things like ads, paintings, photos, and traditional print texts) linked to classroom-ready activities. They also feature a daily document or object via todaysdocument.tumblr.com.

○ "Victorian Infographics" (2009) at the BibliOdyssey blog (bibliodyssey .blogspot.com.au/2009/12/victorian-infographics.html).

- "'Where Children Sleep': A Round-the-World Tour of Bedrooms" (2011) by Maria Popova in *The Atlantic* explores kid interior design across the globe (theatlantic.com/international/archive/2011/08 /where-children-sleep-a-round-the-world-tour-of-bedrooms/243303).

FILM/TV

- *10 Buildings That Changed America* (2013) directed by Roger M. Sherman is a tour of ten influential works of architecture and their cultural impacts.

- *Antiques Roadshow* on PBS shares the hidden story of the found objects that people uncover in their lives (pbs.org/wgbh/roadshow).

- *Bill Cunningham New York* (2010) directed by Richard Press. This documentary features the octagenarian *New York Times Style Section* photographer who is obsessed with photographing the way people dress.

- *Cathedrals of Culture* (2014), a long documentary series made up of six shorts by multiple directors (including Robert Redford and Wim Wenders), uses narration so that some of the most famous buildings on the planet "speak."

- *Earth: A New Wild* (2015) directed by Nicolas Brown. This nature series hosted by conservationist M. Sanjayan explores humans' relationships with the wildest places on Earth.

- *Food Inc.* (2008) directed by Robert Kenner explores the myths and hazards of our industrial food system.

- *Frank Lloyd Wright* (1998) directed by Ken Burns and Lynn Novick. This documentary takes viewers inside the life and creative achievements of famous Midwestern architect Frank Lloyd Wright.

- *Gasland I* (2010) and *Gasland II* (2013) directed by Josh Fox explore the impact of hydraulic fracturing ("fracking") for gas in American communities.

- *History Detectives* on PBS is a television series dedicated to "exploring the complexities of historical mysteries" with a team of expert History Detectives. The show researches artifacts ranging from a Bob Dylan guitar possibly used at the Newport Folk Festival in 1965 to a copperhead cane that inspired a political movement against Abraham Lincoln. The show's website (pbs.org/opb/historydetectives) has an educational section with a series of "activity packs" and behind-the-scenes resources.

- *The History of Toys and Games* (1997), A&E Television Networks. Hosted by actor John Ritter, this documentary takes a look at toys from ancient civilizations through the virtual reality toys emerging in the late 1990s.

○ *Just for Kicks* (2006) directed by Lisa Leone and Thibaut de Longeville. This documentary is about the ascent of sneakers from B-Boy accessory to the bedrock of hip-hop fashion, fueling a $26 billion global market.

○ *King Corn* (2007) directed by Aaron Woolf explores the monoculture of corn and its impact on the American diet.

○ "Lost Buildings" (2004) by Ira Glass, Chris Ware, *This American Life,* and Public Radio International (store.thisamericanlife.org/ProductDetails .asp?ProductCode=LOSTBUILDINGSBOOKDVD). This story is about a young Chicago boy who in the 1960s and '70s becomes obsessed with old buildings—especially those of prominent Chicago architects that were then being torn down. This radio narrative comes to life with illustrations by graphic novelist Chris Ware on this fascinating DVD.

○ National Geographic's TV series *Party Like* (natgeotv.com.au/tv/party-like) began in 2012 with episodes available for streaming online. This show offers a unique approach to cultural history by taking viewers behind the scenes of the "biggest, the most excessive, and the most outrageous parties the world has ever known."

○ "Dr. Sarah Ganz on Object-Based Learning" (2010) from the Rhode Island School of Design Museum of Art (youtube.com/watch?v= A4j78ixyUoo)

○ *Objects and Memory* (2008) directed and produced by Jonathan Fein is a PBS documentary that explores stories of items recovered or offered to the filmmaking team after the terrorist attacks of September 11, 2001.

○ *Olympia*: *The Complete Original Version* (1936) directed by Leni Riefenstahl is a highly stylized, groundbreaking, and controversial documentary about the 1936 Olympics in Nazi-controlled Berlin.

○ *Parts Unknown* hosted by Anthony Bourdain uses food as a way to explore little-known cultures (cnn.com/shows/anthony-bourdain-parts-unknown).

○ *Sketches of Frank Gehry* (2005) directed by Sydney Pollack is a feature documentary about the groundbreaking Canadian American architect Frank Gehry, known for his explosive free-form structures like the Guggenheim Museum in Bilbao, Spain; the Walt Disney Concert Hall in downtown Los Angeles; and the MIT Stata Center in Cambridge, Massachusetts.

○ *The Story of Stuff* (2007) directed by Louis Fox is available on YouTube. This twenty-minute documentary about the lifecycle of material goods raises questions about the sustainability of the American lifestyle.

○ *Valentino: The Last Emperor* (2008) directed by Matt Tyrnauer. This fly-on-the-wall feature documentary about Italian fashion designer Valentino Garavani follows him as he prepares for a retrospective exhibit celebrating his career in Rome.

○ *Years of Living Dangerously* (2015), produced by Daniel Abbasi, Joel Bach, James Cameron, David Gelber, Arnold Schwarzenegger, and Jerry Weintraub, is an Emmy Award–winning nine-part TV series that explores the dramatic challenges and impacts of global warming across the planet.

In humanities classes it is very engaging to use LEOs to explore objects depicted in a story or a work of art from a specific time period to see what they can tell us about a society. The trick here is to remember to treat things that seem frivolous in academic settings, like shoes, fashion, or the design of someone's bedroom, as texts worthy of time and attention. Each of these objects tells the "story of us" at different junctures of civilization.

In STEM classes students often forget that math and science are all around us. Almost every major city has a science museum like Chicago's Museum of Science and Industry (msichicago.org /education), and New York City now has a Museum of Mathematics (MOMATH). No matter where you find artifacts, we feel that it is useful to give students imagery without labels when doing LEOs so that they can uncover ideas about what these images might represent. One of our favorite books to cut up for class (using a used copy we obtained online) is Yann Arthus-Bertrand's *Earth from Above*. Each image illustrates the intricate relationship humans have with the planet.

Games

Playground, Sports, Board, Online, Role Plays, Simulations, and Video

Mindblue Twitter List: twitter.com/_mindblue_/lists/mcpop-games
Twitter Hashtags: #arlearning (augmented-reality learning), #gbl (game-based learning), #mediaed, #medialit, #digitalit, #seriousgames, #sportsociety

In *Reality Is Broken* (2011) Jane McGonigal defines a game as "an activity with goals, rules, a feedback system, and voluntary participation." Games can take many forms, from playground games to sports to board games to text-based simulations or elaborate virtual worlds inhabited by many players. Whatever type of game you explore, students are generally excited to analyze these texts.

Some Useful LEOs

Archivist, Blogger, Casting Director, Detective, Gamer, Highlighter, Hypothesizer, Mood Catcher, Predictor, Producer, Soundtrack Supervisor, Summarizer, Tech Specialist, Wild Card, Wonderer, Worldviewer

Starting Points

BOOKS

- *The Art of Game Design: A Book of Lenses* (2008) by Jesse Schell. Schell is a former Disney game designer and now professor at Carnegie Mellon. This book breaks down his ideas about how an effective and meaningful game is created.

- *Gaming the Past: Using Video Games to Teach Secondary History* (2011) by Jeremiah McCall. This book provides practical ideas for using simulations in class to develop critical thinking and historical literacy.

- *Gaming the World: How Sports Are Reshaping Global Politics and Culture* (2010) by Andrei S. Markovits and Lars Rensmann explores the global language of sport and its impact on daily life around the globe.

- *How Soccer Explains the World: An Unlikely Theory of Globalization* (2010) by Franklin Foer uses the global pastime as a metaphor for the 21st century.

- *Flip Flop Fly Ball* (2011) by Craig Robinson explores baseball through a series of infographics.

- *Mathematics Education for a New Era: Video Games as a Medium for Learning* (2011) by Keith Devlin. Devlin is a math professor at Stanford University and the "Math Guy" on NPR. This book makes a compelling case for the use of computer games as an essential tool for engaging math pedagogy.

○ *The Multiplayer Classroom: Designing Coursework as a Game* (2010) by Lee Sheldon. Sheldon, a college professor, explains how he designed courses as a game mimicking the structures of popular video games.

○ *A People's History of Sports in the United States: 250 Years of Politics, Protest, People, and Play* (2009) by Dave Zirin takes the tone of his blog "The Edge of Sports" to chronicle larger-than-life sporting characters and contests to tell an alternative history of America, a la Howard Zinn.

○ *Playing to Learn: Video Games in the Classroom* (2007) by David Hutchison. Hutchison, a teacher educator, shares a wide variety of practical ideas and examples for sharing video games across the fourth-through twelfth-grade curriculum.

○ *Reality Is Broken: Why Games Make Us Better and How They Can Change the World* (2011) by Jane McGonigal. TED Talks sensation Jane McGonigal shows how we can harness the power of gaming to tackle a wide range of social challenges.

○ *Student-Designed Games: Strategies for Promoting Creativity, Cooperation, and Skill Development* (2010) by Peter A. Hastie. This book is a guide for teachers interested in working with students to create physical games as collaborative learning projects.

○ *Sports in American Life: A History* (2011) by Richard O. Davies gives a groundbreaking history of sports culture in America.

○ *A Theory of Fun for Game Design* (2004) by Ralph Koster. This book is designed to help game designers think narratively about their work while making games engaging and fun.

○ *Video Games and Learning: Teaching and Participatory Culture in the Digital Age* (2011) by Kurt Squire. This book begins by looking at the valuable concepts and skills that can be learned through video games and ends discussing how they might shape the future of education.

○ *What Video Games Have to Teach Us About Learning and Literacy* (2007) and *Good Video Games and Good Learning* (2007) by James Paul Gee. Gee is a linguist whose recent academic work explores how video games develop literacies. These books are essential resources for those who want academic justification and research for the use of video games in the classroom.

WEBSITES

○ Center for Games and Impact at Arizona State University (gamesand impact.org). The mission of this center is to be a hub for researchers, game developers, and entrepreneurs to use computer and video games to create sustainable solutions for social, cultural, scientific, economic, and educational challenges.

o The Center for Sport, Peace, and Society at the University of Tennessee–Knoxville's College of Education, Health, and Human Sciences is a collaboration between the University of Tennessee and the nonprofit organization Sport 4 Peace; it works to use sport as a way to build strong and resilient communities (sportandpeace.utk.edu/about/#philosophy).

o *Contested*, an NPR series produced by John Biewen (of the Center for Documentary Studies at Duke University), presents stories on the role of sports in the lives of young people and their families (stateofthereunion.com/contested).

o The Center for Game Science at the University of Washington (centerforgamescience.org) uses games to solve the hard problems facing humanity. The focus of their game creation and research is to find optimal learning pathways for STEM education through collective intelligence.

o The Computer and Video Game Archive (CVGA) at the University of Michigan Library (lib.umich.edu/computer-video-game-archive) actively collects classic game consoles, computers, games, and related materials for academic study.

o The Education Arcade (educationarcade.org) was established by leading scholars of digital games and education at MIT. Presently this organization partners with a variety of media companies to research and develop educational games.

o ESPN, "the worldwide leader in sports" network, is ripe with long and short texts for student analysis and discussion (espn.go.com). See also Derek Thompson's 2013 article in *The Atlantic* "The Global Dominance of ESPN" (theatlantic.com/magazine/archive/2013/09/the-most-valuable-network/309433).

o Evoke (urgentevoke.com) is a Web game developed by the World Bank Institute and Jane McGonigal. Players receive weekly missions by reading and then investigating comic narratives around real-world "missions." Topics include things like food and water security, energy, disaster relief, poverty, and education. Each module asks students to "evoke" changes and solutions in the real world.

o Games for Change (gamesforchange.org) is a nonprofit creator and distributor of games that leverage entertainment and engagement for social good. This site contains links to their games on myriad social issues and houses the Games for Change Festival.

○ The Games for Learning Institute at New York University (g4li.org) researches how theory and practice can design powerful educational games to enhance learning.

○ Games + Learning + Society Collective in the Educational Communications and Technology program at the University of Wisconsin–Madison (gameslearningsociety.org) is a collective of academic researchers, interactive text developers, and government and industry leaders looking at how learning systems, such as schools, might utilize these types of participatory cultures.

○ Game Salad (gamesalad.com) and Game Star Mechanic (gamestarmechanic.com) are two examples of online game creation tools to help people learn game design and create games using digital templates.

○ The Gaming Group at Making Curriculum Pop (mcpopmb.ning.com /group/gaminginschool) is a social network forum for teachers to share questions and resources about integrating gaming into the classroom.

○ Hopscotch (gethopscotch.com and available at the Apple app store) is a drag-and-drop app that allows students to create their own video games.

○ Interactive Communications and Simulations at the University of Michigan (Flint and Ann Arbor) (ics.soe.umich.edu) has served K–college learning communities for over thirty years, developing a "dynamic assortment of Web-based programs harnessing the power of simulation gaming, activism, service learning and social networking for educational purposes."

○ The *New York Times* Learning Network video games lesson plans (learning.blogs.nytimes.com/tag/video-games) and sports lesson plans (learning.blogs.nytimes.com/tag/sports) use a wide range of *Times* content. Print articles are emphasized, but they also explore images, video, and infographics and supply a wide range of graphic organizers for educators to explore current gaming and sports stories while connecting teachers with additional archive content.

○ Quest 2 Learn School (q2l.org) and the related Institute of Play (instituteofplay.org) were founded by Katie Salen, a game designer, animator, and design educator. This national charter school network is built around using game play in multiple forms to guide inquiry and project-based learning.

FILMS/VIDEOS

NOTE: Video games are now a more profitable industry than films. Given that fact, it is interesting that few films about the medium are produced and widely distributed in traditional forms. However, there are many short-subject and niche films about games and gaming available on the Web. Here are some available on DVD and Web essentials.

○ *16 Days of Glory* (1986) directed by Bud Greenspan dramatically chronicles the stories of multiple Olympians as they compete for gold at the 1984 Los Angeles Olympics.

○ *Bend It Like Beckham* (2002) directed by Gurinder Chadha is a fiction film about the daughter of an orthodox Sikh who tries to escape her controlling parents by going from England to Germany with a football (soccer) team.

○ *Blue Crush* (2002) directed by John Stockwell is a surfer film based on the *Outside* magazine article "Life's Swell" by Susan Orlean. The film tells the story of three teen girls who dream of surfing on Hawai'i's North Shore.

○ *Breaking Away* (1979) directed by Peter Yates is a comedy exploring a group of high school buddies who challenge the local college boys in the town's annual bike race.

○ ESPN's *30 for 30* documentary film series (espn.go.com/30for30) explores watershed sports stories and themes that speak to issues in the broader culture.

○ *Indie Game: The Movie* (2012) directed by Lisanne Pajot and James Swirsky. This documentary follows indie game developers on their journey from concept to release.

○ *Friday Night Lights* (2004) directed by Peter Berg is a fiction film that profiles the role of high school football in the depressed town of Odessa, Texas. Also made into a popular TV series that aired from 2006 to 2011.

○ Jane McGonigal's TED Talk "Gaming Can Make a Better World" is available at ted.com and forms the basis of her book *Reality Is Broken*. Her work is built around creating games that make players activists who work to solve real-world problems.

○ Kurt Squire, director of the Games + Learning + Society Collective at the University of Wisconsin–Madison, gives a short talk on the connection between video games, learning, and civic participation (vimeo.com/21214156).

○ *King of Kong: A Fistful of Quarters* (2007) directed by Seth Gordon. This quirky documentary takes viewers inside the competitive gaming culture, as an upstart Donkey Kong player breaks the record set in 1982 by the "gamer of the century" Billy Mitchell.

○ *Game Over: Gender, Race & Violence in Video Games* (2010) directed by Nina Huntemann; available from the Media Education Foundation (mediaed.org). Although this film was produced in 2010, the topics and issues raised are equally relevant to present-day gamers. The film's website includes a study guide and transcript for classroom use.

○ *Miracle* (2004) directed by Gavin O'Conner is a fictionalized telling of the 1980 U.S. Olympic men's hockey team's unlikely path to gold.

○ The PixelProspector website is a resource site for game developers. They also maintain "The Big List of Video Game Documentaries" (pixelprospector.com/i-history-of-video-games) for those interested in digging deep into the medium online.

○ *Race to World First* (2011) directed by Zachary Henderson and John Keating. This documentary captures the struggles of a twenty-five-person World of Warcraft team as they battle over twelve million players across the planet in an attempt to beat the newest bosses of the game. The film explores the rivalries and life/game conflicts behind their quest.

○ *Video Game Invasion: The History of a Global Obsession* (2004) directed by David Carr and David Comtois. This documentary uncovers the history and designers behind the development of the multibillion-dollar gaming industry.

○ *War Games* (1983) directed by John Badham. This thriller is about a high school hacker and his girlfriend who manage to take control of the government computer system designed to defend the United States against a nuclear attack from the Soviet Union. The lines between games and reality blur as the student and the government frantically work to prevent thermonuclear warfare.

○ *When We Were Kings* (1996) directed by Leon Gast is an Oscar-winning documentary about the 1974 heavyweight championship in Zaire between champion George Foreman and underdog challenger Muhammad Ali.

○ Wikipedia has an amazing "List of Sports Films" from 1925 to present sorted by year and sport (en.wikipedia.org/wiki/List_of_sports_films).

In humanities classes LEOs can be used to analyze games in the same way one might look at a film. Students can make observations on the design, characters, plot, conflicts, and sociological portrayals. Additionally, students can design video games using tools like those provided by Scholastic's Level Up website (scholastic.com/createvideogames). Then students can use LEOs as criteria to analyze each other's games.

In STEM classes we enjoy using games like Spore (spore.com) that deal with scientific content—in this case evolution—where one set of students plays the games and another group of students analyzes their decisions using LEOs. The same can be done for math games. As an example, math teachers might use the game World of Warcraft. You can see models of these practices at the World of Warcraft in School Wiki (wowinschool.pbworks.com/w /page/5268731/FrontPage).

Moving Image: Fiction

TV, Online, Short, and Feature

Mindblue Twitter List: twitter.com/_mindblue_/lists/mcpop-mi-fiction
Twitter Hashtags: #arted, #artsed, #cinema, #cinemaed, #filmed, #mediaed

A fiction film is any story told via moving images that is completely made up or a fictionalization of a true story. Fiction film contains many subgenres including, but certainly not limited to, comedy, horror, science fiction, romance, drama, and thriller.

It is worth noting that most things based on or inspired by a true story are still considered fiction because of the dramatic license used to create the story. A movie like the 2010 Academy Award winner *The King's Speech* is based on historical events, but the theatrical nature of the narrative and the way it was presented fall clearly within the fiction film genre.

The term *film* can be a bit of a misnomer, as many professional and amateur films are now shot using digital camera or hybrids (where people shoot on film and transfer it to digital formats for editing). New technologies allow people to view fiction films anywhere a screen is available.

Some Useful LEOs

Archivist, Blogger, Body Linguist, Cartoonist, Casting Director, Designer, Detective, Dialogue Master, Fashion Critic, Gamer, Genre Guru, Geographer, Hypothesizer, Mood Catcher, Producer, Sensor, Soundtrack, Summarizer, Supervisor, Time Catcher, Timeliner, Wonderer, Worldviewer

Starting Points

BOOKS

- *Celluloid Blackboard: Teaching History with Film* (2006) edited by Alan S. Marcus. This collection explores frameworks, scholarship, and practices of using film in the secondary history classroom.

- *Great Films and How to Teach Them* (2004) by William V. Costanzo. The first section of this book gives secondary and college teachers frameworks for the teaching of film as stand-alone texts. The second half contains short essays and study guides for fourteen classic films.

- *Mastering Media Literacy* (2014) edited by Heidi Hayes Jacobs. This book is part of a larger literacy series, makes the case for a rich cinema-based curriculum.

- *Reading in the Dark: Using Film as a Tool in the English Classroom* (2001) by John Golden. Golden guides English teachers through ways to use film as stand-alone texts while making links to traditional literacy practices. The book contains over thirty case studies, graphic organizers, and a glossary of film terms.

- *Reel Conversations: Reading Films with Young Adults* (1996) by Alan B. Teasley and Ann Wilder. While this book is older, it remains—in our opinion—one of the most thoughtful books about how and why to teach film to young learners. We use the text in our graduate classes for teachers to understand films using a critical eye.

- *Teaching History with Film: Strategies for Secondary Social Studies* (2010) by Alan S. Marcus, Scott Alan Metzler, Richard J. Paxton, and Jeremy D. Stoddard. This book presents models for the effective use of film to develop historical literacies in social studies classrooms. Themes include development of historical empathy, development of interpretive skills, and the exploration of controversial historical issues.

- *Teach Science with Science Fiction Films: A Guide for Teachers and Library Media Specialists* (2004) by Terence Cavanaugh and Cathy Cavanaugh. This book is a strong starting point for science teachers looking to connect sci-fi with traditional science curricula.

- *Understanding Movies* (get the latest edition) by Louis Giannetti. This college textbook is our personal favorite for teachers interested in getting a comprehensive understanding of the art, business, craft, and theory of film and filmmaking.

WEBSITES

- The Academy of Motion Picture Arts and Sciences Teachers' Guide series (oscars.org/education-outreach/teachersguide/index.html). Each downloadable guide in the series focuses on different film disciplines: Animation, Art Direction, Costume Design, Costumes & Makeup, Documentaries, Film Editing, Screenwriting, Sound & Music, and Visual Effects.

- The American Film Institute's "100 Years . . ." (afi.com/100years). AFI works with the film industry to create these Top 100 lists of American films. These are excellent for teachers looking to find canonical/critically acclaimed films, and they are also fun to give to students to guide independent viewing projects.

- The British Film Institute has an Education and Research department (bfi.org.uk/education-research) with many resources, including their Screenonline guide (screenonline.org.uk), an educational supplement. The BFI also publishes a Teaching Film and Media Studies series (palgrave.com/series/teaching-film-and-media-studies/BFITFMS).

- The Film Canon Project (filmcanonproject.com) is linked to the aforementioned Heidi Hayes Jacobs book *Mastering Media Literacy*. This collaborative site is designed for educators to shape and debate a film canon for educators.

- The Film Foundation's Story of Movies (storyofmovies.org). Martin Scorsese created the Film Foundation to preserve historically and artistically significant films. Their mission expanded into film education, partnering with IBM and Turner Classic Movies to create the educational curriculum for classic American films. They are now beginning to create resources for international films, starting with the Introduction to Contemporary Chinese Film resource guides and activity booklets (goo.gl/XRn74).

- The Internet Movie Database (imdb.com) is the Web's largest free film information directory. This is a great place to search for basic information about a film. You can find information on a film's cast, crew, and shooting locations. You can also use the site to link to critics' reviews and even search for movies around themes and keywords using their Movie Keyword Analyzer (MoKA) (imdb.com/Sections/Keywords).

- iTunes Short Film store (itunes.apple.com/us/genre/movies-short-films/id4414) and Shorts: The Short Movie Channel (shorts.tv) are excellent places to search for short-subject films by themes, keywords, and countries.

○ The London Film Museum (londonfilmmuseum.com) is funded by the film industry to present exhibits and films about the art, history, and craft of filmmaking. This young museum supports an education department whose online resources are evolving.

○ The Museum of the Moving Image (movingimage.us) in Brooklyn, New York, is dedicated to "the art, history, technique and technology of the moving image in all its forms." The education tab on their website includes information on teacher programs and curated online resources for classroom use.

○ The "Teach with Moving Images" (mcpopmb.ning.com/group /teachwmovies) and the "Foreign Films for the Classroom—Non English" (mcpopmb.ning.com/group/foreignfilmsfortheclassroom) and "Digital Storytelling" (mcpopmb.ning.com/group/digitalstorytelling) groups at Making Curriculum Pop are social network forums for teachers to share questions and resources about integrating the moving image into classroom practice.

○ The *New York Times* Learning Network Film Lesson Plans (learning .blogs.nytimes.com/tag/film), as well as the TV and video lesson plans, use a wide range of *Times* content. Print articles are emphasized, but they also explore images, video, and infographics and supply a wide range of graphic organizers for educators to explore current film, TV, and video stories while connecting teachers with additional archival content.

○ Teach with Movies (teachwithmovies.org) is a subscription-based website that has over 350 learning guides for movies commonly taught in K–college. Their approach is more traditional than ours in this book, but each learning guide is comprehensive and contains resources, extensions, and questions to help develop learning experiences around film.

○ The Museum of Broadcast Communications (museum.tv) in Chicago also hosts the Radio Hall of Fame (radiohof.org). This institution collects, preserves, and presents historic and contemporary radio and television content. In addition to their extensive archives, their education department curates materials and develops teaching resources for classroom use.

○ The Paley Center for Media (paleycenter.org) has locations in New York City and Los Angeles and was originally called the Museum of Television and Radio but was renamed in 2007 to reflect a wider range of media. Both locations have searchable archives and educational departments that work with K–college teachers and students at every level.

FILMS

○ *Basic Film Terms: A Visual Dictionary* (1971) (pyramidmedia.com /homepage/search-by-title/humanities/basic-film-terms-detail.html). We find it somewhat shocking that this instructional film has not been remade. A staple of film and media classes for over forty years, this product of four young filmmakers uses short, silly sequences to demonstrate a wide variety of film terms. Although a handful of terms are outdated, this is still a classic teaching film.

○ *The Bronze Screen: 100 Years of the Latino Image in American Cinema* (2002) directed by Nancy De Los Santos, Alberto Domínguez, and Susan Racho. This documentary casts a critical and celebratory eye on the past, present, and future of Latinos in motion pictures.

○ *The Celluloid Closet* (1993) directed by Rob Epstein and Jeffery Friedman is a unique documentary that features top talents investigating Hollywood's treatment of homosexual characters in the 20th century.

○ *The Cutting Edge—The Magic of Movie Editing* (2004) directed by Wendy Apple. This documentary is simultaneously a history on the art of film editing and a master class. Top editing, acting, and directing talents share examples from movies to illustrate the power of "final cut."

○ *The Dialogue: Learning from the Masters* series available from the Writers Store in Los Angeles (writersstore.com/the-dialogue-learning-from-the-masters). Each DVD features interviews of top Hollywood screenwriters. Great for teachers interested in helping students learn the craft of screenwriting and also valuable if you want to hear from a writer of a film that you are teaching.

○ *Directors: Life Behind the Camera* (2006) produced by the American Film Institute. Over 300 hours of interviews with top American directors are edited into a feature-length documentary about life behind the director's chair.

○ *The Hold Up: An Editing Exercise with Roger Ebert* (1983) directed by Stephen Hank and Barbara Coleman (firstlightvideo.com). This instructional video is hosted by film critic Roger Ebert. Viewers are taken through the shooting of a "hold-up" sequence and then shown various ways the footage can be edited to create different meanings. While students may initially smile at the now-unfashionable hair and jeans of the actors, this short remains an essential illustration of the power of editorial choices.

- *Inside the Actors Studio* DVDs (1994–present). Shown on the Bravo cable television channel in the United States, this show brings top national and international acting (and sometimes directing) talent to the stage for extensive interviews about their art and craft.

- *A Personal Journey with Martin Scorsese through American Movies* (1995) directed by Martin Scorsese and Michael Henry Wilson. This documentary is not a standard history of cinema but instead Scorsese's individual experience of film history. While many canonical films are discussed, many lesser-known films and directors are introduced to viewers.

- *Reel Injun: On the Trail of the Hollywood Indian* (2009) directed by Neil Diamond. This documentary explores Hollywood's on- and offscreen relationships with indigenous peoples.

- *These Amazing Shadows* (2011) directed by Paul Mariano and Kurt Norton gives viewers a tour of the films added to the Library of Congress's National Film Registry.

- *Visions of Light: The Art of Cinematography* (1993) directed by Arnold Glassman, Todd McCarthy, and Stuart Samuels. This film is out of print but is still available used. This documentary traces the history and art of cinematography, illuminating the visual language of light.

- *Valentino's Ghost* (2011) directed by Michael Singh. Available from Bullfrog Films (bullfrogfilms.com), this film looks at the way images of Arabs and Muslims in movies and on television have shifted in concert with American politics.

In humanities classes we enjoy using films that develop students' general background knowledge about a time period or an issue and allow for comparisons between fact and fiction. In the language arts, we have found Golden Age television shows like *I Love Lucy* and *The Twilight Zone* (aligned to clear teaching objectives) and grade-level-appropriate sports films to be rich, especially if you're teaching the heroic journey. The fine arts can use LEOs for careful analysis of things such as set design, music, costumes, dancing, or acting.

In STEM classes we enjoy using films that develop students' background knowledge about an issue. We find that science fiction films can be incredible teaching tools. For example, the Arnold Schwarzenegger film *The 6th Day* is an outstanding resource if you want to teach about the ethics of animal, human, and plant cloning or DNA manipulation and the ethical challenges of those topics. To get ideas for STEM-related films, see the Blick on Flicks reviews from the National Science Teachers Association website (nsta.org/publications/blickonflicks.aspx) and the Museum of the Moving Image's Sloan Science and Film website (scienceand film.org/about), and search for math sequences/clips at the Mathematics and Movies website (math.harvard.edu/~knill /mathmovies) or the Math and the Movies Resource List (math bits.com/MathBits/MathMovies/ResourceList.htm). Use these clips or features with LEO roles to uncover student questions and ideas around STEM concepts.

Moving Image: Nonfiction

Documentaries, Reality Shows, and Network TV

Mindblue Twitter List: twitter.com/_mindblue_/lists/mcpop-mi-nonfiction
Twitter Hashtags: #arted, #artsed, #cinema, #cinemaed, #docfilm, #filmed, #mediaed, #movingimage

Nonfiction film and TV are commonly referred to as documentaries. This genre is an attempt to capture a reality or truth. In this objective record of a factual truth the viewer must carefully sort out facts, omissions, and points of view to make determinations about a film's content. Many documentary filmmakers will stage events that capture the spirit of the truth, leaving many complex questions for students to explore.

This genre includes most broadcast news, TV, and film documentaries, as well as a wide range of reality television, although their "reality" can be suspect. As with fiction film, you can immerse yourself in this genre any-where you find a screen.

Some Useful LEOs

Archaeologist, Blogger, Cartoonist, Data Analyst, Demographer, Economist, Fact Checker, Framer, Gamer, Hypothesizer, Lawyer, Predictor, Producer, Sociologist, Time Catcher, Timeliner, Wonderer, Worldviewer

Starting Points

BOOKS

○ *The Art of the Documentary: Ten Conversations with Leading Directors, Cinematographers, Editors and Producers* (2005) by Megan Cunningham. This book features a series of interviews and captures documentary filmmakers sharing their thoughts on the process, methods, and collaborations behind the creation of documentary films.

○ *How to Watch TV News* (1992) by Neil Postman and Steve Powers. Postman started his career as a secondary English teacher and developed into an advocate of an ecological approach to media. In this book Postman and Powers discuss the big business behind local and national television news.

○ *A New History of Documentary Film* (2005) by Betsy A. McLane. This text is a chronological exploration of the development of documentary film. One unique element of the book is its emphasis on archival and preservation history, as well as issues of copyright and fair use.

○ *Reading in the Reel World: Teaching Documentaries and Other Nonfiction Texts* (2003) by John Golden. Golden's follow-up to *Reading in the Dark* (2001) is designed for teachers of all disciplines looking to explore validity, objectivity, and bias in nonfiction texts.

○ *Reality Bites Back: The Troubling Truth About Guilty Pleasure TV* (2010) by Jennifer L. Pozner. Media critic Pozner deconstructs the powerful messages about gender, race, class, sexuality, and consumerism portrayed in reality TV and how they shape cultural discourse.

○ *Teaching Film and TV Documentary* (2008) by Sarah Casey Benyahia is part of the British Film Institute's Teaching Film and Media Studies series. The book includes rationales, approaches, and case studies for teaching documentaries.

WEBSITES

○ *Documentaries to See Before You Die* (mubi.com/lists/current-tvs-50-documentaries-to-see-before-you-die) was a television show on Current TV hosted by acclaimed documentary filmmaker Morgan Spurlock. The list showcases the "best" documentaries produced from 1985 to 2010. While the list is open for debate, it is a great starting point for anyone looking to understand the art and recent history of documentary film in America.

- The Academy of Motion Picture Arts and Sciences Teachers' Guide series: see entry in the Moving Image: Fiction section.

- The British Film Institute's Education & Research department resources: see entry in the Moving Image: Fiction section.

- Comedy Central's flagship fake news programs *The Daily Show* (thedailyshow.com), *The Nightly Show* (nightlyshow.com), and *The Colbert Report* (colbertnation.com) are available online. The shows do an exemplary job of deconstructing mainstream media using video clips as fuel for their intellectual satire. Teachers can use their "video clip" tab and search by keywords.

- *Independent Lens* on PBS (pbs.org/independentlens) is an Emmy Award–winning television series that brings independent documentary film to public television. Some films are streamed online and also have a "classroom" tab on their site (pbs.org/independentlens/classroom) filled with lesson plans, activities, and film modules for individual films.

- The International Documentary Association (documentary.org) is a nonprofit organization for documentary filmmakers and fans. The site features clips from longer documentaries and their affiliated *Documentary* magazine with excellent features about documentaries in wide release as well as lesser-known productions.

- iTunes Documentary films (itunes.apple.com/us/genre/movies-documentary/id4405) and Shorts: The Short Movie Channel (shorts.tv) are excellent places to find short-subject films by themes, keywords, and countries. Many of the recent Oscar-nominated Short Subject Documentaries are available at these sites. Wikipedia has a comprehensive list of nominees and winners to get you started: en.wikipedia.org/wiki/Academy_Award_for_Best_Documentary_(Short_Subject).

- The Media That Matters Film Festival (goo.gl/xYCN36) presented by Arts Engine is now defunct, but they have an outstanding collection of social-justice-themed "short films that inspire action."

- Lesson plan ideas from the *New York Times* Learning Network (learning.blogs.nytimes.com/tag/documentary-film) use Snag films and a wide range of *Times* content. Print articles are emphasized, but they also explore images, video, and infographics and supply a wide range of graphic organizers for educators to explore documentary films in every discipline while connecting teachers with additional archival content.

- The Television News Archive at Vanderbilt University (tvnews.vanderbilt.edu) allows you to search newscasts from major networks and cable television from the presidency of Lyndon Baines Johnson to the present day. Once you find clips you might be interested in teaching with, you can request a loan from the collection or pay for a DVD of a broadcast you are interested in viewing.

○ The "Teach with Moving Images" (mcpopmb.ning.com/group /teachwmovies), "Foreign Films for the Classroom" (mcpopmb.ning .com/group/foreignfilmsfortheclassroom), and "Digital Storytelling" (mcpopmb.ning.com/group/digitalstorytelling) groups at Making Curriculum Pop are social network forums for teachers to share questions and resources about integrating the moving image into classroom practice.

○ The Museum of Broadcast Communications in Chicago also hosts the Radio Hall of Fame. See entry in Moving Image: Fiction section.

○ The Paley Center for Media. See entry in Moving Image: Fiction section.

○ The London Film Museum. See entry in Moving Image: Fiction section.

○ The Museum of the Moving Image. See entry in Moving Image: Fiction section.

FILMS—DOCUMENTARY

NOTE: There are vast numbers of quality documentaries. The following films are either essential documentaries (often dealing with media issues) or fiction films about the presentation of "real events" in visual mediums.

○ *5 Broken Cameras* (2011) directed by Emad Burnat and Guy Davidi. This documentary follows a Palestinian farmer's nonviolent resistance to the Israeli army.

○ *Bowling for Columbine* (2002) directed by Michael Moore. This Academy Award–winning film is a critical exploration of the school shootings at Columbine High School and the media's response to those events at the end of the 20th century.

○ *The Civil War* (1990), directed by Ken Burns. This film was so influential that there is now a film term commonly used on slide shows called the "Ken Burns effect." This PBS series documenting the American Civil War is expansive and unique in the way it presents historical events.

○ *Control Room* (2004) directed by Jehane Noujaim. This documentary is about the Qatar-based television news network Al Jazeera and its relationship with U.S. Central Command during the 2003 invasion of Iraq.

- *Gasland* (2010) and *Gasland Part II* (2013) directed by Josh Fox. This pair of films is a deeply personal exploration of the effects of hydraulic fracturing (aka "fracking") across the United States.

- *In Search of the Edge: An Inquiry into the Shape of the Earth and the Disappearance of Andrea Barns* (1990) directed by Scott Barrie. This brilliant short documentary available from Bullfrog Films (bullfrogfilms .com) is constructed to prove a well-researched "flat earth" point of view while painting the "global earth" doctrine as a hoax. The film is designed to help students think critically about stories as presented in visual texts.

- *Hoop Dreams* (1994) directed by Steve James. This documentary was shot over the course of five years as the director followed two middle school basketball stars into adulthood as they pursued their dreams of playing in the National Basketball Association (NBA). Although the film was snubbed by the Academy Awards, in 2007 this film was named the greatest documentary of all time by the International Documentary Association (documentary.org/content/top-25-docs).

- *NOVA: The Great Math Mystery* (2015) directed by Dan McCabe and Richard Reisz. This TV documentary explores the timeless question "Is math invented by humans, or is it the language of the universe?"

- *Outfoxed: Rupert Murdoch's War on Journalism* (2004) directed by Robert Greenwald. This documentary is a left-leaning exposé that mimics the visual tactics of Fox News to criticize the right-leaning network.

- *Triumph of the Will* (1935) directed by Leni Riefenstahl. Riefenstahl was given carte blanche by Hitler to document and help plan the 1934 Nazi Party Congress in Nuremberg. This propaganda was wildly innovative and, given its influence, is an excellent case study on the line between documentary and propaganda.

- *When the Levees Broke: A Requiem in Four Acts* (2006) directed by Spike Lee. Lee and his team traveled to New Orleans, Louisiana, shortly after the levees failed during Hurricane Katrina. Mixing news footage with comprehensive interviews, this project will become more important over time. Teachers College at Columbia University partnered with HBO and Lee to create an extensive set of teaching tools and curriculum to support teaching the documentary at the website Teaching *The Levees* (teachingthelevees.org) that includes multimedia tools, essays, and downloadable lesson plans.

FILMS—FICTION ABOUT REAL-WORLD ISSUES

- *The China Syndrome* (1979) directed by James Bridges. A film that remains timely in light of the 2011 Fukushima Daiichi power plant disaster in Japan, this film follows a television news reporter and her cameraman who discover cover-ups of safety violations at a nuclear power plant.

- *Good Night and Good Luck* (2005) directed by George Clooney. This biopic focuses on the conflict between television journalist Edward R. Murrow and U.S. Senator Joseph McCarthy of Wisconsin and the senator's anti-communist investigations.

- *The Insider* (1999) directed by Michael Mann. This Academy Award–nominated fiction film is about a research chemist who decides to appear on a television exposé of the tobacco industry. The complicated interplay between the whistleblowing chemist (Russell Crowe) and the television producer who wants the story (Al Pacino) gives insights into the challenges of investigative reporting.

- *Network* (1976) directed by Sidney Lumet. This Academy Award–winning satirical film is about a news anchor who snaps under the pressure of poor ratings and begins speaking his true feelings to his audience.

- *The Newsroom* (2012), various directors. This HBO television series goes behind the scenes at a fictional cable news show looking to push back at corporate and commercial pressures.

In humanities classes, we find it interesting to teach with and about nonfiction films because they always have a point of view and are shot in a way to support that point of view, so it is critical to deconstruct this for understanding. Fortunately, LEOs allow you to look simultaneously at the art and content of any nonfiction film. A propaganda film like *Triumph of the Will*—despite its positive portrayal of Hitler—is considered important for its artistic innovations. LEOs can help sort out fact, opinion, and bias as you use documentary films as primary sources to explore major historical events.

In STEM classes we recommend using news or documentary clips involving data or statistics. Using LEOs like the Wonderer, Data Analyst, and Fact Checker, students can gain better understanding of numbers as a language. In a film like *Bowling for Columbine,* inquisitive students will see how Michael Moore may at times choose to use raw numbers and at other times percentages to advance his argument. A documentary about climate change like *An Inconvenient Truth* was hotly (pun intended) debated at its release. LEOs allow students to assess claims made in films to research and assess them for fairness and accuracy. As students see more films that use statistical or numerical data, they inevitably come up with questions about research methods and data collection. LEO roles like the Predictor, Data Analyst, or Sensor can help students hypothesize what happens next, based on the data presented.

Music

The Art, Craft, and Business of Live and Recorded Music

Mindblue Twitter List: twitter.com/_mindblue_/lists/mcpop-music
Twitter Hashtags: #artsed, #musicedchat, #musiced, #mused

As an art form, music uses an arrangement of silence and sound to create meaning. Recorded music is a relatively new phenomenon; originally music was a performance art that could only be heard live. With the advent of digital music players, every genre of music is more portable than ever and readily available for classroom exploration.

Some Useful LEOs

Archivist, Blogger, Imagery Hunter, Mood Catcher, Hypothesizer, Wonderer, Worldviewer

Starting Points

BOOKS

○ *The Anthology of Rap* (2010) edited by Adam Bradley and Andrew DuBois. This volume collects more than 300 lyrics spanning over thirty years. The book divides compositions into historical periods, framing the rich and vital poetry of hip-hop culture.

- *Book of Rhymes: The Poetics of Hip Hop* (2009) by Adam Bradley. Bradley, a literary scholar, makes a powerful argument for hip-hop artists as some of the greatest innovators of modern American poetry.

- *From Dylan to Donne: Bridging English and Music* (2003) by Charles B. Dethier. This book presents rationales, examples, and strategies for teachers to connect reading, writing, and thinking to popular music.

- *Hip Hop Genius: Remixing High School Education* (2011) by Samuel Steinberg Seidel. Going far beyond the basic study of popular music and hip hop, this book talks about using the ethos of hip hop to reinvent the "how" of teaching.

- *Musicophilia: Tales of Music and the Brain* (2007) by Oliver Sacks. Neurologist Sacks uses case studies of exceptional individuals to illustrate and illuminate the effects of music on our brains and bodies.

- *Pop-Culture Pedagogy in the Music Classroom* (2010) edited by Nicole Blamonte. This is a collection of essays and lessons for incorporating popular cultures into the music classroom. With lessons around texts like *Guitar Hero* and *American Idol*, teachers in other disciplines can use this as a springboard for cross-curricular applications of popular music.

- *The Popular Music Teaching Handbook: An Educator's Guide to Music-Related Print Resources* (2004) edited by B. Lee Cooper and Rebecca A. Condon. This book guides secondary and college instructors to locate teaching materials and scholarship for teachers in every discipline.

- *Rock and Roll: A Social History* (2006) by Paul Friedlander. Used in many college survey courses about popular music, this popular text explores the history and social impacts of rock and roll and its offspring. This text also introduces Friedlander's "Rock Window," a tool for analyzing rock songs. Consider looking at this tool to inspire some LEO remixes.

- *This Is Your Brain on Music: The Science of a Human Obsession* (2007) by Daniel J. Levitin. Rocker-turned-neuroscientist Levitin explores the how and why of music as it relates to emerging brain research.

- *Top Tunes for Teaching: 977 Song Titles and Practical Tools for Choosing the Right Music Every Time* (2005) by Eric P. Jensen. This book combines brain-based learning principles with music playlists designed to engage students in meaningful learning.

WEBSITES

- The All Music Guide (allmusic.com) is the ultimate resource for music researchers and fans. This site probably contains the most music reviews on the planet, and their writing is often licensed to sites like iTunes and eMusic. Their database also allows one to search by artist, album, song, and even narrower categories like songwriters and musician.

○ Deconstructing the Beatles (beatleslectures.com) is home to musician and educator Scott Freiman, who travels the country giving a multi-media lecture series, breaking down the complex stories behind some of the most famous Beatles songs.

○ Seattle's EMP Museum (empmuseum.org) was formerly known as the Experience Music Project and Science Fiction Museum and Hall of Fame. They currently curate historical and experiential materials about popular music and science fiction. EMP hosts a wide variety of educational programs and curricular resources under the Education tab on their website.

○ Flocabulary (flocabulary.com) is a company that creates original hip-hop music to teach common K–12 academic content through song.

○ The Grammy Museum at L.A. Live (grammymuseum.org) in Los Angeles, California, is a joint effort between the Recording Academy, responsible for the Grammy Awards, and AEG, a music and sports promoter. The museum is designed to be an interactive experience and also hosts a diverse selection of downloadable teacher curricula and resources under their site's Education tab.

○ Jazz at Lincoln Center (jazz.org) and affiliated Nesuhi Ertegun Jazz Hall of Fame (academy.jazz.org/hall-of-fame) are both housed in New York City. JALC hosts a series of podcasts and videos (academy.jazz.org /media-library) where they interview top jazz musicians about their craft and also support an education department.

○ Learning from Lyrics (learningfromlyrics.org) is a nonprofit created by classroom teacher Jonathan Chase to help teachers use songs in all subject areas. While this site may not have the slickest layout, don't pass it up, as it is a treasure trove of resources. You can also get interesting updates through Chase's Facebook group (facebook.com/groups /71704526084).

○ LitTunes (littunes.com) is an educational outreach directed by Christian Z. Goering, a professor of secondary English/literacy education at the University of Arkansas. The site is loaded with rationales, a database of connections between music and literature, lesson plans, and other resources for language arts teachers.

○ Mindblue's Rock and Roll Learning Experience Organizers (mindblue .com/store) are a small but interesting series of study guides created around the work of artists like Jimi Hendrix, Stevie Wonder, and Radiohead for use in humanities classrooms.

○ The "Music Group" at Making Curriculum Pop (mcpopmb.ning.com /group/ popularmusic) is a social network forum for teachers in every discipline to share questions and resources about integrating music into the classroom.

○ The *New York Times* Learning Network music lesson plans (learning .blogs.nytimes.com/category/lesson-plans/fine-arts/music) use a wide range of *Times* content. Print articles are emphasized, but they also explore images, video, and infographics and supply a wide range of graphic organizers for educators to explore current music stories while connecting teachers with additional archive content.

○ The Progressive Arts Alliance's Rhapsody Hip-Hop Education Program (paalive.org/rhapsody.html) is a Cleveland-based nonprofit program dedicated to connecting the arts and technology. The PAA professional development and Rhapsody Hip-Hop program are strong models for the interdisciplinary study of music, arts, and digital media incorporating state and national standards.

○ "The Record" with Ann Powers on NPR (npr.org/blogs/therecord) is a blog built around contributions to NPR news shows that does an excellent job of analyzing and contextualizing the world of popular music. One of their most interesting features (especially for language arts and social studies educators) is the "Sounds of Your American Dream" series, where prominent writers and listeners explore songs that embody their American dream.

○ The Rock and Roll Hall of Fame and Museum (rockhall.com) in Cleveland, Ohio, develops a wide variety of educational programs including their annual Summer Teacher Institute. Their website also hosts over fifty diverse interdisciplinary lessons for K–12 teachers interested in integrating music across the curriculum (rockhall.com /education/resources/lesson-plans).

○ Smithsonian Folkways Tools for Teaching (folkways.si.edu/tools_for_ teaching/introduction.aspx) is an educational site with geotagged lessons and activities built around historical music recordings spanning the globe, shared through the Smithsonian Folkways record label.

○ The Green Book of Songs thematic database (SongsAbout.com) allows educators and music professionals to search for songs by themes and keywords.

FILMS/VIDEOS

○ *American Roots Music* (2001) directed by Jim Brown. This four-episode PBS series takes an in-depth look at genres like bluegrass, blues, country, folk, gospel, and spirituals with historical footage and contemporary interviews. The series' website contains a vast collection of teacher resources and lessons (pbs.org/americanrootsmusic/pbs_arm_into_the_classroom.html).

○ *The Blues: Presented by Martin Scorsese* (2003), various directors. This PBS series is a collection of twelve feature-length films that capture the essence of the blues as an art form and illustrate its global impact. The series' website contains a vast collection of teacher resources and lessons (pbs.org/theblues/classroom.html).

○ *Broadway: The American Musical* (2004) directed by Michael Kantor. This six-part PBS series narrated by Julie Andrews follows the development of the art from vaudeville, operetta, and minstrel shows to the creation of the modern American musical. The series' website contains a vast collection of teacher resources and lessons (pbs.org/wnet/broadway/teachers.html).

○ *Cadillac Records* (2008) directed by Darnell Martin. This highly fictionalized biopic of Chess Records' luminaries includes such names as Leonard Chess, Willy Dixon, Chuck Berry, Little Walter, Muddy Waters, Howlin' Wolf, and Etta James. This story chronicles the rise of the blues from the Mississippi Delta to the South Side of Chicago.

○ *Downloaded* (2013) directed by Alex Winter is a journey into the digital downloading revolution and its impact on bands and the music business.

○ *High Tech Soul: The Creation of Techno Music* (2006) directed by Gary Bredow. This documentary reveals the evolution of techno framed by a cultural history of Detroit.

○ *The History of Rock and Roll* (1995) directed by Andrew Solt. This ten-episode series take a wide-angle view on the creators, innovators, and icons of popular music into the late 20th century.

○ *Jazz: The Story of American Music* (2001) directed by Ken Burns. This ten-episode PBS series is a survey of the musical form, its innovators, and stars from its New Orleans beginnings. The series' website contains a vast collection of teacher resources and lessons (pbs.org/jazz/classroom).

○ *Lady Sings the Blues* (1972) directed by Sidney J. Furie. This biopic chronicles the rise and fall of legendary blues singer Billie Holiday.

○ *The Music Instinct: Science and Song* (2009) directed by Elena Mannes. This two-hour PBS documentary follows researchers and musicians through the mysterious intersections of science, culture, and music.

○ *NOVA* "Musical Minds with Dr. Oliver Sacks" (2010) directed by Louise Lockwood. This is a fascinating exploration of the vital power of music in the lives of four people with extreme health challenges.

○ *Ray* (2004) directed by Taylor Hackford. This Academy Award–winning biopic follows the breakthrough career and struggles of international R&B sensation Ray Charles.

○ *Scratch* (2002) directed by Doug Pray. This documentary traces the development of turntables into an essential instrument for hip-hop artists.

○ *Something from Nothing: The Art of Rap* (2012) directed by Ice-T and Andy Baybutt focuses on the "old school," early days of rap by interviewing prominent rappers and MCs about their craft.

○ *Walk the Line* (2005) directed by James Mangold. This biopic explores the early life and career of country musician Johnny Cash and his rise to fame.

In humanities classes you can find a lot of music that directly correlates to your content. For example, explore this blog about rock songs written about historical events: mademan.com/mm/10-rock-songs-written-about-historical-events.html. Or you can use music like the work of Woody Guthrie (zinnedproject.org/posts/18581) or a song that had historical, social, or political impact (see timeout.com/london/feature/1488/100-songs-that-changed-history-the-full-list) as a primary source document to study a time period. It is also easy to find songs with thematic links to an artwork you might be studying. For example, if you do a close reading of Faith Ringgold's narrative about city living, *Tar Beach,* you can enhance student engagement and connections by pairing it with Stevie Wonder's famous song "Living for the City."

In STEM classes one can also find many songs that directly correlate, like the classic *Schoolhouse Rock* series (see the *Schoolhouse Rock: Science Classroom Edition* DVD released by Disney in 2008), the They Might Be Giants album *Here Comes Science* (2009), or the tunes of Mr. Duey (mrduey.blogspot.com). You can also find music or music videos that deal explicitly with numbers, like Sarah McLachlan's "World on Fire" video, or you can have students listen to a song like the Rihanna single "Man Down" paired with an NPR story on *Planet Money,* "How Much Does It Cost to Make a Hit Song?" (npr.org/blogs/money/2011/07/05 /137530847/how-much-does-it-cost-to-make-a-hit-song). You can assign certain LEOs for the song and others for the radio story.

Newspapers and Magazines

Print and Digital

Mindblue Twitter List: twitter.com/_mindblue_/lists/mcpop-newspapers-mags

Twitter Hashtags: #journalism, #newsed, #magazine, #mediaed

Newspapers and magazines are often referred to collectively as periodicals. Most are supported by advertising revenue. Magazines tend to have a content focus (fashion, movies, sports), while newspapers typically have sections (arts, business, news) but also make space for proceedings of legislative bodies and public notices. Today, many periodicals are distributed in print and digital forms, often redesigning their formats for e-readers and tablets. Some newspapers have folded in the face of Internet competition. Others, like the *Ann Arbor News,* reinvented themselves as a digitally delivered product: the newspaper, which closed in 2009 after 174 years in business, has morphed into the website AnnArbor.com. It still publishes a weekly print edition under the new title, making the line between periodical and website blurred.

Some Useful LEOs

Archaeologist, Archivist, Cartoonist, Demographer, Economist, Fact Checker, Framer, Highlighter, Hypothesizer, Lawyer, Producer, Timeliner, Time Catcher, Wonderer, Wordsmith, Worldviewer

Starting Points

BOOKS

- *The Art of Making Magazines: On Being an Editor and Other Views from the Industry* (2012) edited by Victor S. Navasky and Evan Cornog. This anthology features art directors, editors, publishers, and writers from prominent magazines like *The New Yorker, Elle,* and *The New Republic* commenting on industry challenges. The book is based on a lecture series at the Columbia University School of Journalism.

- *Front-Page Science: Engaging Teens in Science Literacy* (2011) by Wendy Saul, Angela Kohnen, Alan Newman, and Laura Pearce. This book, published by the National Science Teachers Association (NSTA), offers teachers a rationale for the use of journalism in science, explores case studies, and guides teachers through science journalism projects for their students. The book has an accompanying website (teach4scijourn .org) where authors and teachers share lesson plans and ideas.

- *Infamous Scribblers: The Founding Fathers and the Rowdy Beginnings of American Journalism* (2007) by Eric Burns is an engaging narrative about the Founding Fathers' relationship to early America journalism as it was defining itself.

- *Investigative Journalism: Proven Strategies for Reporting the Story* (2008) by William C. Gaines. This how-to guide is written for new investigative journalists using case studies presented by the Pulitzer Prize–winning author.

- *Lesson Plans for Creating Media-Rich Classrooms* (2007) edited by Mary T. Christel and Scott Sullivan. This teacher-created anthology from the National Council of Teachers of English contains lesson plans for every media type, including ones on newspaper and magazine analysis and production.

- *The Magazine Century* (2010) by David E. Sumner. This history charts the rise of the magazine in the 20th century in the context of social, cultural, and economic trends.

- *Muckrakers: How Ida Tarbell, Upton Sinclair, and Lincoln Steffens Helped Expose Scandal, Inspire Reform, and Invent Investigative Journalism* (2007) by Ann Bausum. This middle school book is a succinct introduction to some of the journalists who reshaped American media in the early 20th century.

- *The New New Journalism: Conversations with America's Best Nonfiction Writers on Their Craft* (2005) by Robert S. Boynton. This book explores the "New New Journalist," those influenced by the reporting of Tom Wolfe, Hunter S. Thompson, and Gay Talese. Boynton interviews nineteen writers about their methods, writing, and careers.

- *Personal History* (1998) by Katharine Graham. This Pulitzer Prize–winning memoir mixes *Washington Post* publisher and owner Katharine Graham's personal history with American history.

- *Telling True Stories: A Nonfiction Writer's Guide from the Nieman Foundation at Harvard University* (2007) edited by Mark Kramer and Wendy Call. This book collects brilliant talks (turned into essays) by top nonfiction writers like Nora Ephron, David Halberstam, Susan Orlean, and Malcolm Gladwell.

- *unSpun: Finding Facts in a World of Disinformation* (2007) by Brooks Jackson and Kathleen Hall Jamieson. This book comes from the founders (one a journalist, the other an academic) of the popular website FactCheck.org out of the Annenberg Public Policy Center of the University of Pennsylvania. This book helps readers spot spin, see common tricks of deception, and ultimately find trustworthy news sites.

WEBSITES

- The Association of Magazine Media (magazine.org) is an organization designed for magazine publishers, but their site is an excellent resource for students and educators looking to research the business of magazines.

- The Center for News Literacy at Stony Brook University (centerfornewsliteracy.org) was founded by the dean of the School of Journalism to develop news literacy on campus as well as in secondary and postsecondary schools across the United States. They also host an annual conference for educators to share and develop best practices.

- Columbia Scholastic Press Association (CSPA) (cspa.columbia.edu) is based at the Columbia University Graduate School of Journalism in New York City. This organization holds conventions, workshops, and award contests for student editors and faculty advisors in K–12 schools producing newspapers, magazines, yearbooks, and online text.

- High School Newspaper (facebook.com/pages/Mikes-High-School-Newspaper/179359238766695) is an online newspaper sponsored by Michael Moore. His stated objective is to give students an open forum where high school students can share their thoughts and ideas with millions as they submit blogs, music, and videos to be shared at the paper.

○ Journalism Education Association (jea.org), based at Kansas State University, is a scholastic journalism organization for journalism teachers and publication advisors. The site includes curricular resources, their magazine, and professional development opportunities.

○ The "Journalism Teachers" (mcpopmb.ning.com/group/journalism teachers), "Magazines" (mcpopmb.ning.com/group/magazines) and "The News: Teaching with and about It" (mcpopmb.ning.com/group /teachingwithaboutthenews) groups at the Making Curriculum Pop Ning are part of a social network forum for teachers to share questions and resources about integrating journalism into the classroom.

○ The Knight-Wallace Fellows at Michigan (mjfellows.org) and the Neiman Foundation for Journalism at Harvard (nieman.harvard.edu) are two organizations that grant fellowships to journalists, hold events, and share resources around issues and emerging best practices in journalism. While their educational work is not geared toward secondary teachers, they are both excellent resources for educators interested in emerging challenges, issues, and practices in the field.

○ The Newseum (newseum.org) in Washington, D.C., is an interactive space covering more than five centuries of news history with the latest technologies. They have a wide range of educational programming and curricular resources for teachers under the Education tab at the site. One of their most exciting resources is their daily front-page gallery showcasing hundreds of front pages from all over the world for student comparison and study (newseum.org/todaysfrontpages).

○ The News Literacy Project (thenewsliteracyproject.org). Founded by a Pulitzer Prize–winning journalist and investigative reporter, this project develops collaborations between practicing journalists and teachers to help secondary students develop understandings and standards for truthful and reliable information.

○ The *New York Times* Learning Network (learning.blogs.nytimes.com) and more specifically the *New York Times* Learning Network journalism lesson plans (learning.blogs.nytimes.com/category/journalism) use a wide range of *Times* content. Print articles are emphasized, but they also explore images, video, and infographics and supply a wide range of graphic organizers for educators to explore current events and journalism while connecting teachers with additional archive content.

○ The Poynter Institute (poynter.org) and the Poynter News University (newsu.org) are two branches of a professional organization that teaches and trains those who blog about, edit, design, manage, photograph, or report news. The News University includes materials for K–12 educators.

○ The Zinn Education Project (zinnedproject.org) is built around the ideas articulated in historian Howard Zinn's writings and ideas about a "people's history." Many teaching materials at the site include primary source documents, such as accounts from newspapers and periodicals.

FILM AND VIDEO

○ *American Experience* episode "Around the World in 72 Days" (1997) directed by Mel Bucklin and Christine Lesiak. This PBS documentary is a portrait of Nellie Bly (Elizabeth Cochrane Seaman), the first female "stunt" journalist who immersed herself in her stories. The film focuses on her attempt to beat the record set by the fictional hero of Jules Verne's novel *Around the World in 80 Days* (1873).

○ *All the President's Men* (1976) directed by Alan J. Pakula. This Academy Award–winning dramatization of *Washington Post* reporters Bob Woodward and Carl Bernstein's book of the same name shows the investigative work of two young reporters whose reporting ultimately helped bring down President Nixon in the early 1970s.

○ *Citizen Kane* (1941) directed by Orson Welles. Considered by many to be the greatest film of all time, it is a fiction film with parallels to the rise and fall of newspaper magnate William Randolph Hearst at the beginning of the 20th century.

○ *Crucible of Empire: The Spanish American War* (2007) directed by Daniel A. Miller. This film examines the events that shaped the 1898 war, including the infamous "yellow journalism" practices of publishers William Randolph Hearst and Joseph Pulitzer.

○ *Final Edition* (2009) is a short film about the final days of the *Rocky Mountain News,* a 149-year-old newspaper. Available online at vimeo.com/3390739.

○ *Frontline* episode "Murdoch's Scandal" (2012) produced by Lowell Bergman. This hour-long documentary follows the phone hacking and bribery scandals that brought down Rupert Murdoch's tabloid *News of the World* in the United Kingdom. The struggle for the future of News Corporation is the subject of the latter half of the documentary, as filmmakers follow the British Parliamentary inquiry in London. This episode streams online (pbs.org/wgbh/pages/frontline/murdochs-scandal), is available for download at iTunes, or can be ordered as a DVD from PBS.

- *The Devil Wears Prada* (2006) directed by David Frankel. A classic comedy about a naive young woman who becomes an assistant to a high-powered—and ruthless—fashion magazine editor.

- *His Girl Friday* (1940) directed by Howard Hawks. This screwball romantic comedy follows a newspaper editor who pulls out all the stops to keep his star reporter—and ex-wife—from remarrying. While the film is more of a romance, it mimics the feel of mid-century newsrooms.

- *Page One: Inside the* New York Times (2011) directed by Andrew Rossi. With access to the *New York Times* newsroom navigating stories during a transformational moment in media, this documentary is a complex exploration of one of the most vital newspapers in the world.

- *The Paper* (1994) directed by Ron Howard. This comedy follows the life of a workaholic editor at a New York tabloid who considers taking a more respectable job at a traditional newspaper to spend more time with his children. As the story unfolds, the protagonist is forced to make some hard choices.

- *Shattered Glass* (2003) directed by Billy Ray. A dramatization of the real-life scandal of Stephen Glass, a D.C.-based magazine reporter who fell from grace after fabricating a series of articles.

- *State of Play* (2009) directed by Kevin Macdonald; based on the BBC TV series of the same name (2003) directed by David Yates. This TV show and its film adaption show investigative reporters working parallel to a police detective to discover who murdered the mistress of a member of Parliament/member of Congress. Both works nicely illustrate the complicated interconnections between the public, law enforcement, government, and media.

- *Tell the Truth and Run: George Seldes and the American Press* (1995) by Rick Goldsmith, available at newday.com. This Academy Award–nominated documentary studies the career of Seldes, a muckraking journalist whose reporting was the subject of great controversy and censorship. His career spanned much of the 20th century, and viewers visit revolutions, fascism, cover-ups, and witch hunts with the reporter who spent a career attempting to "tell the truth, and run."

In humanities classes, have students focus on content, layout, design, and selection of text and image. We love using LEOs with the Newseum's daily collection of front pages (newseum.org /todaysfrontpages). Students don't always need to be able to read the news they are exploring. You can assign groups to different non-English geographic regions and they can explore each culture and its news visually.

In STEM classes books like *Front-Page Science: Engaging Teens in Science Literacy* (2011) are springboards for LEOs that can be used to acquaint students with excellent scientific journalism from magazines like *National Geographic, Smithsonian, Wired, Popular Mechanics,* and *Scientific American* to support literacy across the curriculum.

Social Networks/Web 2.0

Blogs, Webpages, Wikis, Nings, Facebook, and Twitter

Mindblue Twitter List: twitter.com/_mindblue_/lists/mcpop-soc-net-web-2-0
Twitter Hashtags: #edtech, #elearning, #smchat (social media chat), #smedu (social media and education)

The *Internet* and *social networks* are terms that describe the massive, online, multimedia universe. *Web 2.0* is a term used to describe the collaborative and interactive uses of the Internet epitomized by tools like Facebook, Twitter, and Ning. The only common denominator of these tools is that they are all presented digitally via computers, handheld devices, tablets, and other emerging technologies.

Some Useful LEOs

Archivist, Connector, Data Analyst, Demographer, Fact Checker, Highlighter, Producer, Tech Specialist, Summarizer, Web Master, Wonderer, Wordsmith, Worldviewer

Starting Points

BOOKS

○ *Authentic Learning in the Digital Age: Engaging Students Through Inquiry* (2015) by Larissa Pahomov. This book, written by a teacher at Philadelphia's Science Leadership Academy, gives examples of student work around five core values.

○ *Digital Tools for Teaching: 30 E-Tools for Collaborating, Creating, and Publishing Across the Curriculum* (2011) by Steve Johnson. This book is an elegant how-to guide for teachers looking to explore the latest technologies in classrooms. Using succinct summaries and guides for each e-tool, Johnson gives teachers a range of extension ideas in every discipline.

○ *Media Literacy, Social Networking, and the Web 2.0 Environment for the K–12 Educator* (2011) by Belinha S. De Abreu. This book uses the ideas of media literacy to frame discussion about the effective uses of social media in the K–12 classroom.

○ *Personal Learning Networks: Using the Power of Connections to Transform Education* (2011) by Will Richardson and Rob Mancabelli. This book explains the power of online personal learning networks (PLNs). After explaining to educators how and why they can connect with PLNs, the authors guide teachers in the creation of classroom- and school-level PLNs.

○ *Rethinking Education in the Age of Technology: The Digital Revolution and Schooling in America* (2009) by Allan Collins and Richard Halverson. This book explores the effects of the digital revolution inside and outside of school and makes a case for radical reinvention of school systems.

○ *The Socially Networked Classroom* (2009) and *The Global School: Connecting Classrooms and Students Around the World* (2012) by William Kist. In these two texts, Kist takes a national and then international look at the ways social networks are changing K–12 classroom practices. He uses case studies to develop criteria for effective networked classrooms.

○ *So You've Been Publically Shamed* (2015) by John Ronson explores the historical antecedents for online shaming and how one tweet can ruin a person's life.

○ *Trust Me, I'm Lying: Confessions of a Media Manipulator* (2012) by Ryan Holiday. The author of this book went from college dropout to master media PR man and manipulator. This complicated book (especially given the title) explores how social media and blogs have altered the landscape for marketers and journalists.

○ *Web 2.0: New Tools, New Schools* (2007) and *Web 2.0: How-To for Educators* (2010) by Gwen Solomon and Lynne Schrum. Both of these texts guide teachers though powerful digital tools and how they might be used to explore content and develop critical literacies in the classroom.

WEBSITES

NOTE: When we write *closed network* we mean that these resources are designed for in-school networking only and, while there may be options to share the work of students on larger platforms, generally these networks are for localized teacher, student, and parent eyes only. Closed networks have drawbacks, but they do an excellent job of addressing Internet safety concerns because they do not allow for open networking. In general, our feeling is that the younger the student, the more beneficial a closed network can be, but it all depends on your district's technology and networking policies.

- 21 Classes Cooperative Learning (21classes.com) is a closed network site designed for the creation of closed network teacher and student blogs.

- Classroom 2.0 Ning (classroom20.com). This Ning social network has, as of this printing, almost 70,000 teachers across the globe collaborating around Web 2.0 and social media in the classroom. They also host an annual online Social Learning Summit.

- Edmodo (edmodo.com) is a social network for educators who want to create Facebook-like closed networks for their school community. Pam uses Edmodo to communicate with her students, who enjoy the daily interaction.

- Edublogs (edublogs.org) is a site like Blogger designed to allow the creation of closed networks for school communities. Since 2004, Edublogs has hosted annual Edublog Awards (edublogawards.com) to honor exemplary uses of online media in the classroom in almost twenty categories. The present winners and previous winners tabs allow teachers to research some of the best online blogs, networks, tweeters, podcasts, wikis, social networks, and apps for educators.

- Epals Global Community (epals.com) is a closed network to help teachers all over the planet match students with pen pals by classroom or project.

- The Global Education Conference Ning (globaleducationconference.com) is a global social network for educators at all levels designed to increase opportunities for collaborative education while supporting cultural awareness and diversity. The group hosts a free weeklong online education conference in the fall via Blackboard Collaborate.

- Facebook in Education (facebook.com/education) is a Facebook group that shares resources, success stories, and tips for integrating Facebook into curriculum.

○ The Joan Ganz Cooney Center at Sesame Workshop (joanganzcooneycenter.org) is dedicated to answering the question, "How can digital media help children learn?" The center is a hub of research and initiatives emphasizing new literacies in early education, intercultural understanding, media literacy, and advancing science, technology, engineering, and math (STEM).

○ MacArthur Foundation's Digital Media and Learning programs and grantmaking (macfound.org/programs/learning) support research and practices around the ways young people learn, play, socialize, and participate in civic life online. Their work also links to a series of reports published by the MIT Press on digital media and learning (scribd.com /collections/2346520/John-D-and-Catherine-T-MacArthur-Foundation-Reports-on-Digital-Media-and-Learning).

○ The "New Media and Technology" group at Making Curriculum Pop (mcpopmb.ning.com/group/newmediatechnology) is a social network forum for teachers to share questions and resources about integrating new media and technologies into the classroom.

○ The *New York Times* Learning Network technology lesson plans (learning.blogs.nytimes.com/category/technology) use a wide range of *Times* content. Print articles are emphasized, but they also explore images, video, and infographics and supply a wide range of graphic organizers for educators to explore online technologies while connecting teachers with additional archive content.

○ Project New Media Literacies (newmedialiteracies.org) at the USC Annenberg School for Communications and Journalism is a Ning community spearheaded by professor Henry Jenkins. This project is built around developing understandings of learning in the context of participatory cultures.

○ Will Richardson's blog (willrichardson.com) uses the tag "Read. Write. Connect. Learn." Richardson was one of the early public educators to write about his practices integrating new technologies into his personal and district teaching practices. Considered a leader in the connected learning community, his work is a strong starting point for educators interested in using the Web for collaborative learning.

FILMS/VIDEOS

○ *Catfish* (2010) directed by Henry Joost and Ariel Schulman. This documentary unfolds like a thriller, as the directors watch a mysterious online friendship develop between the filmmaker's brother and a young woman.

○ Edutopia's video library from the George Lucas Educational Foundation (edutopia.org/video) is a rich resource for teachers looking for short films about teachers and their students using new technologies in the classroom. You might start your search using the technology integration category and your grade level of interest.

○ *In Plain English* videos by Common Craft are animations explaining tech topics like blogs, protecting reputations online, secure websites, Twitter and Twitter search, social bookmarking, social media, social networking, Web search strategies, wikis, and Wikipedia. All of these are available on YouTube and TeacherTube and can be searched at Common Craft's website (commoncraft.com/#all-videos).

○ *Frontline* episodes (pbs.org/wgbh/pages/frontline/) "Growing Up Online" (2008) and "Digital Nation" (2010) directed by Rachel Dretzin, and "Generation Like" (2014) written by Frank Koughan and Douglas Rushkoff. These three *Frontline* documentaries explore the pros and cons of online and digital cultures.

○ *Terms and Conditions May Apply* (2013) directed by Cullen Hoback investigates what corporations and governments learn about people through the Internet.

○ *The Social Network* (2011) directed by David Fincher. This biopic about Facebook founder Mark Zuckerberg's ascent from Harvard student to billionaire tech mogul is a compelling, if historically complicated, story about the business of social media.

In humanities classes it can be interesting to look "behind the frame" of whatever content you are viewing. The "comment" feature on most webpages is ripe for study using LEOs. You can look at artwork (a short story, music, film, etc.) archived, created, or presented online. Some LEOs can be used to look at the actual art while others can be directed toward the distinctly social comments section. In a similar vein students can assess the reliability of any webpage as a primary source document. Students can also explore Wikipedia pages and their revisions (simply click the View History tab at the top to see discussions). LEO roles like the Archaeologist, Framer, and Lawyer allow students to uncover interesting questions, ideas, and connections about any page. Furthermore, you don't have to limit your activity to one webpage, but can instead have students choose a series of webpages on a historical or current events topic and make assessments about the pages as a whole.

At one point "The Dork Side," a Facebook community page (facebook.com/TheDorkSide1) that posts humor *(not always classroom friendly)*, posted a screen shot of a fourteen-year-old student's comment on a classic Jimi Hendrix performance of "Hey Joe" that has since been removed from YouTube. The student says:

> *"Don't get me wrong. This guy is okay but I'm 14 and I can speak for everyone my age when I say as TIME goes on music gets better and better. We have more technology to make better songs with various sounds and not just the same boring guitar over and over again. Musicians like skrillex and lmfao and even the jonAs brothers have more technology and knowledge at their disposal to make better quality songs."*

If a student discovered a comment like this about Jimi Hendrix using LEOs, we imagine it would be the source of rich discussion and debate. Be sure to screen comments when possible, as there may be content or discussions that might not be appropriate for your classroom.

In STEM classes we find engaging infographics to be ideally suited to make your curriculum pop with LEOs. Some of our favorite infographics are found at *Good Magazine* (good.is/infographics). *The Guardian* (UK) newspaper has a data visualization blog (theguardian.com/data) as does *USA Today* (ftw.usatoday.com/tag /infographics). Many news organizations use Twitter handles to highlight their infographics: see @BBCNewsGraphics (BBC News), @NPRvis (National Public Radio), @nytgraphics (*New York Times*), @PostGraphics (*Washington Post*), @ Reuters Graphics (Reuters) respectively. See the *New York Times* Learning Network (learning .blogs.nytimes.com) posts "Teaching with Infographics—Places to Start" and "Data Visualized: More on Teaching with Infographics" for a wide range of resources to help you explore infographics using LEOs.

You can also use STEM-related Twitter feeds as a text. The February 2014 issue of the *Journal of Adolescent and Adult Literacy* had an article by Mellinee Lesley titled "Spacecraft Reveals Recent Geological Activity on the Moon: Exploring the Features of NASA Twitter Posts and Their Potential to Engage Adolescents" that will give you ideas about how a Twitter feed can become fodder for LEOs.

Visual Arts

Drawing, Graphic Design, Painting, Photography, Sculpture, and Mixed Media

Mindblue Twitter List: twitter.com/_mindblue_/lists/mcpop-visual-arts
Twitter Hashtags: #arted, #artsed, #museumed, #vised, #vislit, #visualliteracy

Visual arts is a catch-all term here for the types of art you might see in galleries, museums, and public spaces. Nontraditional visual art such as graffiti art or computer art also fits in this category, along with traditional practices such as drawing, graphic design, painting, photography, sculpture, and mixed-media creation. This category focuses on visual works created with artistic intent to capture moments, ideas, or feelings.

Obviously, advertisements, comics, and television are also visual arts, but they are not talked about as frequently as "arts."

In many situations you will be looking at still images of things in magazines, books, posters, museums, or on the Internet, but we hope you will have students capture still images in public spaces when possible. Still images can really be found everywhere! We love to tear up books from discount stores and reflect on what we see.

Some Useful LEOs

Archaeologist, Archivist, Blogger, Designer, Geographer, Hypothesizer, Imagery Hunter, Intuitor, Mood Catcher, Poet, Predictor, Producer, Sensor, Tech Specialist, Timeliner, Wonderer, Worldviewer

Starting Points

BOOKS

○ *Criticizing Photographs: An Introduction to Understanding Images* (2005) by Terry Barrett. This short text is for beginners and advanced students interested in becoming more articulate about describing, interpreting, evaluating, and theorizing about photos.

○ The Captured History Series: *Birmingham 1963: How a Photograph Rallied Civil Rights Support* (2011) and *Little Rock Girl 1957: How a*

Photograph Changed the Fight for Integration (2012) by Shelley Tougas; *Raising the Flag: How a Photograph Gave a Nation Hope in Wartime* (2011) and *Breaker Boys: How a Photograph Helped End Child Labor* (2011) by Michael Burgan; *Man on the Moon: How a Photograph Made Anything Seem Possible* (2011) by Pamela Dell; and *Migrant Mother: How a Photograph Defined the Great Depression* (2011) by Don Nardo. These books are written to take us "behind the scenes" of some of the 20th century's most iconic photos.

○ *How to Read a Painting: Lessons from the Old Masters* (2004) and *How to Read Bible Stories and Myths in Art: Decoding the Old Masters from Giotto to Goya* (2008) by Patrick De Rynck; *How to Read a Modern Painting: Lessons from the Modern Masters* (2006) by Jon Thompson; and *How to Read World History in Art* (2010) by Flavio Febbraro and Burkhard Schwetje. This series beautifully reproduces major artworks accompanied by short essays and nicely explained "close-ups" that help deepen understandings of artworks in context.

○ *I Wanna Take Me a Picture: Teaching Photography and Writing to Children* (2002) by Wendy Ewald. Written before the explosion of digital photography, this book explores the use of film instead of computers for image creation. This interdisciplinary approach puts the images and words of students in the foreground, while giving tips on image composition, darkroom use, and film development.

○ *Teaching Visual Culture: Curriculum, Aesthetics, and the Social Life of Art* (2003) by Kerry Freedman. This book mixes theory and practice for teachers interested in using the ubiquity of visual cultures to craft engaging K–12 curriculum.

○ *Visual Thinking Strategies: Using Art to Deepen Learning Across School Disciplines* (2013) by Philip Yenawine in an excellent introduction to VTS that you can use across the curriculum.

○ *Ways of Seeing* (1990) by John Berger. This book was based on the 1972 BBC Television series of the same name (chunks of this can be seen on YouTube.com). This widely influential book explores the primacy of vision and major ideas about art practice, theory, and criticism through print and visual essays.

○ *Why Is That Art? Aesthetics and Criticism of Contemporary Art* (2011) by Terry Barrett. This is an excellent text for teachers interested in being able to answer the big title question with answers informed by aesthetics, art theory, art criticism, and the philosophy of art.

WEBSITES

- Adobe Education Exchange integrates technology and imagery (edexchange.adobe.com/pages/d4178d15ff).

- The "Art & Visual Cultures" group at Making Curriculum Pop (mcpopmb.ning.com/group/artteachers) is a social network forum for teachers to share questions and resources about integrating art into the classroom.

- The Internet Archive's book images feed on Flickr has put almost three million book images from libraries across the world online (flickr.com /photos/internetarchivebookimages/with/14784850762).

- Museums: many major U.S. and international institutions have wonderful educator resources online. Most museums have lesson plans, reproductions of art, and a wide range of interdisciplinary resources available for educators. We have collected sites from larger museums below; do take some time to explore your favorite local resources online. Because many of the museums in Washington, D.C., have expansive missions, they are highlighted in the Cultural Artifacts section.

  Chicago
  - The Art Institute of Chicago Education Department (artic.edu/learn)
  - DuSable Museum of African American History (dusablemuseum.org/education)
  - Museum of Contemporary Art (MOCA) (mcachicago.org/archive/collection)

  London
  - The National Gallery (nationalgallery.org.uk/learning/teachers-and-schools)
  - The Tate Gallery (tate.org.uk/learn/online-resources)

  Los Angeles
  - The J. Paul Getty Museum (getty.edu/education/teachers)
  - The Museum of Contemporary Art (MOCA) (edu.moca.org/education/teachers)

  New York City
  - El Museo del Barrio (elmuseo.org) explores Latino and Caribbean culture and also shares many of their exhibits online.
  - The Guggenheim (guggenheim.org/new-york/education/school-educator-programs/teacher-resources)
  - International Center for Photography Teacher Resources (icp.org/museum/education/teacher-resources)

- Metropolitan Museum of Art's Teacher Resources
  (metmuseum.org/events/teachers)
- Museum of Modern Art's Modern Teacher Resources
  (moma.org/modernteachers)
- Studio Museum Harlem (studiomuseum.org)

San Francisco
- Asian Art Museum (education.asianart.org)
- De Young Museum of Fine Arts
  (deyoung.famsf.org/education/k-12-students-0)
- San Francisco Museum of Modern Art (SFMOMA)
  (sfmoma.org/explore/educators/teacher_resources)

○ The *New York Times* Learning Network fine arts lesson plans (learning
.blogs.nytimes.com/category/fine-arts) use a wide range of *Times* content. Print articles are emphasized, but they also explore images, video,
and infographics and supply a wide range of graphic organizers for
educators to explore current fine arts stories while connecting teachers
with additional archive content. You can also explore more specific tags
like photography (learning.blogs.nytimes.com/tag/photography) and
painting (learning.blogs.nytimes.com/tag/painting).

FILMS

○ *Art21* is a television and online film series from PBS (pbs.org/art21).
Since premiering in 2001, this show documents the work of contemporary artists all over the world. Under the Learn tab at the site, you can
find a series of printable resources for teachers (pbs.org/art21
/learning-with-art21/materials-for-teaching).

○ *Born into Brothels* (2004) directed by Zana Briski and Ross Kauffman;
see also kids-with-cameras.org/bornintobrothels. This Academy Award–
winning documentary chronicles photographer Zana Briski's trips to
the red-light districts of Calcutta (Kolkata), India. Initially there to
photograph child prostitutes, she ultimately befriended these children
and taught them how to capture their lives on film. This work led Briski
to found Kids with Cameras, a nonprofit that teaches photography to
marginalized children throughout the world.

○ *Colored Frames: A Visual Art Documentary* (2007) directed by Lerone D.
Wilson and available through Amazon and boondogglefilms.com. This
documentary looks back at fifty years of African-American art from the
height of the civil rights movement into the early 21st century.

○ *Half Past Autumn—The Life and Works of Gordon Parks* (2006) directed by Craig Rice. Parks embodies the Renaissance man as a photographer, poet, novelist, composer, and filmmaker. This film frames Parks's work as an African-American artist in the context of major historical events.

○ *Maya Lin: A Strong Clear Vision* (1995) directed by Freida Lee Mock. This Academy Award–winning documentary focuses on Lin's striking sculpture and design. The most fascinating part of the film looks back on the controversy behind the Vietnam War Memorial that she designed in Washington, D.C.

○ *Simon Schama's Power of Art* (2006) directed by Clare Beavan, Steve Condie, and Carl Hindmarch. This BBC documentary series is written and hosted by Columbia University professor of history and art history Simon Schama. Each of the show's eight episodes dramatically explores the creation of a masterpiece of painting, sculpture, or design.

In humanities classes, we like to use LEOs with any collection of images that relate to the themes studied in class. We often buy photo books from the bargain section of bookstores, tear them up, and laminate the images so they become "textual manipulatives" that students can share and explore, using LEOs to deeply read them. LEOs can help students understand that images can communicate just as much as a poem or book. We also use images to build background knowledge for a time period. If you're reading *To Kill a Mockingbird,* you might use LEOs to explore images of the 1930s to build background knowledge. A search for editor Nick Yapp at Amazon.com pulls up the now out-of-print (but available used) *Decades of the 20th Century* photo books that are an excellent starting place.

In STEM classes we suggest teachers use still images of fractals, patterns, and structures, as well as the geometric patterns in nature and architecture. Even photos of celebrities might make a powerful learning experience around the idea of the golden ratio. In many science settings we find it useful to give students scientific imagery with or without labels. Starting with pictures of a cell, planets, environments, or animals, students can use LEOs to develop ideas about what these images might represent. One of our favorite books to cut up for class is Yann Arthus-Bertrand's *Earth from Above* series that illustrates the intricate relationship humans have with nature.

CHAPTER 5

LEARNING EXPERIENCE ORGANIZERS (LEOs)

This chapter offers a variety of LEOs to help develop literacy skills across the content areas. After exploring the descriptions of each LEO, you can use whatever combination you think would be useful with any given text. For your reference, pages 134–138 show five student examples of LEOs filled out after watching the film *Rescue Dawn*.

Figure 5.1 LEO Student Example

TIME CATCHER

Octavia E. Butler
Novelist, USA, 1947–2006

The **TIME CATCHER's** job is to carefully look at the language, technology, descriptions, and objects (aka context clues) that create the space, place, and time of a text. In other words, the Time Catcher uses context clues to figure out the setting (time and place) of a text. Please be prepared to share your observations with your group.

"People who think about time travel stories sometimes think that going back in time would be fun because you would have all the information you needed to be much more astute than the people there, when the truth is of course you wouldn't."

EXAMPLE

Name **Callie Wilson**	Objective **define unfamiliar words**
Date **June 3**	Text Description **Film, Rescue Dawn, 2006**

In the space below list 8 clues that allowed you to figure out the time period of the piece you're reading/listening to/viewing.

Context Clue	Information This Gives Us About the Setting
Ripped, dirty, green jumpsuits	This shows that they are hunters or trying to hide from others. The ripped and dirty clothes show they have been on for a while.
Green leafy plants & sun	This shows it is in the middle of a hot summer.
A lot of rain & water, waterfalls	This shows it is taking place in a rainforest or jungle.
Dieter used logs to start a fire.	This shows they are stranded and they need to use what they have to the best of their abilities.
Small boy carrying water	This shows it is in the past because now we don't have to walk to get water.
Dieter hiding in the bushes	This shows he was alone with nowhere to go. He didn't know what to do.
Fought & ate a snake for food	He had nothing else. The military/marines taught him to survive no matter what.
The soldiers who saved him gave him a Butterfinger chocolate bar.	This shows he had to survive off animals and plants to stay alive and hadn't had real food for days and months.

Figure 5.2 LEO Student Example

WORDSMITH

Nora Ephron
Author, Screenwriter, Director,
Producer, USA, 1941–2012

"Reading is everything. Reading makes me feel like I've accomplished something, learned something, become a better person. Reading makes me smarter. Reading gives me something to talk about later on. Reading is the unbelievably healthy way my attention deficit disorder medicates itself."

The **WORDSMITH's** job is to find words that are important, new, puzzling, unfamiliar, or unusual. Jot down words that sound unusual or unfamiliar and look them up or try to figure out the word's meaning from context clues. Please be prepared to discuss your choices with your group.

EXAMPLE

TECH TIP

Consider using the Visual Thesaurus (visualthesaurus.com) or Merriam-Webster's Visual Dictionary (visual.merriam-webster.com) to help you visualize the words.

Name	David Fisher

Objective	define unfamiliar words

Date	June 3

Text Description	Film, Rescue Dawn, 2006

Word	Where in This Text Did You Encounter This Word?	Definition or Picture	What Context Clues Support Your Definition?
leech	When it was raining.		It sucks blood.
torch	After Dieter made the fire.		Holds fire, keeps light.
Americali	When Duane is killed.		Name for American.
Vietcong	Throughout		A Vietnamese soldier
coordinates	When Dieter was being interviewed by the FBI.		Location

Figure 5.3 LEO Student Example

WEB MASTER

EXAMPLE

The **WEB MASTER's** job for this portion of the text is to draw a mind map to show your understanding of the text. Start with what you think is a big or main idea and use shapes to make connections. Please be prepared to share your web with your group.

Larry Page
Computer Scientist, Cofounder & CEO of Google, USA, Born: 1973

"Basically, our goal is to organize the world's information and to make it universally accessible and useful."

Name	Katie Brown	Objective	Create a map of the events
Date	June 3	Text Description	Film, Rescue Dawn, 2006

TECH TIP

You may do this role digitally using Inspiration, Bubbl.us, etc.

Dengler was rescued!

The soldiers are preparing to go to Laos to attack the people there.

Going to a new location to attack North Vietnam.

Duane was killed.

They threw their weapons in a river.

The soldiers ask workers to adjust their materials so that they could be better prepared.

The prisoners finally escape.

Rescue Dawn

The soldiers got in a big huddle and they said to stay safe and come back in one piece.

Planes flew overhead and the guards made the prisoners get back in the shelter.

Dieter Dengler was on a mission where he bombed North Vietnam, but his place ended up getting destroyed and he crashed in North Vietnam.

Dieter Dengler flattened a nail in order to create a key to get all the prisoners out of the handcuffs.

Dieter Dengler was captured by citizens of North Vietnam and was tied to the ground.

North Vietnamese people hear the crash and they run after Dengler who is forced to hide in the jungle.

Figure 5.4 LEO Student Example

SENSOR

Patti Smith
Singer-Songwriter, Poet, and
Visual Artist, USA, Born: 1946

"When I was younger, I felt it was my duty to wake people up. I thought poetry was asleep. I thought rock 'n' roll was asleep."

The **SENSOR's** job is to focus on the way that the colors, textures, lighting, and lines of the text present themselves. While this will most often apply to visual texts, many types of media have textures. For example, the sounds of an electric guitar can create a different texture than that of an acoustic guitar—the former is often loud and bombastic, while the latter is usually organic or peaceful. When you look at a text, what do you notice about the textures? Do they help create a certain feeling or emotion? Please be prepared to share your observations with your group.

EXAMPLE

Name	Justin Smith

Objective	observe the way it looks and feels

Date	June 3

Text Description	Film, Rescue Dawn, 2006

Some sample adjectives you might use: abstract, angular, bold, bumpy, complex, curved, dark, dotted, dramatic, dull, earthy, flat, geometric, high/low angle, light, loose, natural, open, organic, pale, scratchy, short, sketchy, skinny, smooth, soft, solid, straight, strong, ugly, vibrant, violent, wide

Focus (check one)	Description of What You Noticed and Where in the Text	Adjective Describing What You Sensed from This Element and Why
☐ Line ☐ Color ☐ Framing ☐ Space ☐ Texture ☒ Lighting ☐ Shadow ☐ Sounds ☐ Other	The lighting was very dark and scary and it always seems like they are under shade.	Scary because the movie and story is all dark.
☐ Line ☒ Color ☐ Framing ☐ Space ☐ Texture ☐ Lighting ☐ Shadow ☐ Sounds ☐ Other	Everything was a green color or shade.	Natural because they were in a jungle and they didn't have any technology so they had to do things without it.
☐ Line ☐ Color ☐ Framing ☐ Space ☐ Texture ☐ Lighting ☒ Shadow ☐ Sounds ☐ Other	There were always shadows and they were always in shade.	Dark because the jungles and tall trees shaded the ground and the events were really dark and bad.
☐ Line ☐ Color ☐ Framing ☐ Space ☐ Texture ☒ Lighting ☐ Shadow ☐ Sounds ☐ Other	At the end of the movie, everything was light and happy when he was rescued.	Light because he was rescued and that was a good thing so everything was happy.

Figure 5.5 LEO Student Example

WONDERER

Spike Lee
Director, Writer, Producer, Actor, USA,
Born: 1957

"You've really got to start hitting the books because it's no joke out here."

The **WONDERER's** job is to write down questions about the text. After you share those questions with your group, you might talk about your group's responses or barriers that are preventing the group from finding an answer. Be sure to ask at least 6 questions below. Please be prepared to share your questions with your group.

EXAMPLE

Name **Savita Mendez**	Objective **ask questions about things I don't know**
Date **June 3**	Text Description **Film, Rescue Dawn, 2006**

I wondered about . . . because . . . (give details to support your question).

1. How hot did it get in Vietnam because the characters were sweating immensely?

2. How did leeches get on Dieter because he was wearing a shirt and leeches need bare skin?

3. Why did Dieter eat the worms even though he didn't need to?

4. What deadly animals lived in Vietnam jungles because that adds to the danger?

5. How did he tolerate eating a snake because that is absolutely disgusting?

6. How did Dieter feel after getting rescued because I would be jubilant?

ARCHAEOLOGIST

*"I like being fooled by my own thoughts
and being challenged and being found
wrong. And I feel that if I let you in on that
journey, you'll be as surprised as I am."*

The **ARCHAEOLOGIST's** job is to look for content that is buried or not seen. Parts of the text might suggest or hint at larger ideas, issues, and contexts. What do you read between the lines? What do you infer? What background information do you have for better discussion or understanding of the text? What do you feel is noteworthy for discussion? Please be prepared to share your connections with your group.

Name		Objective	
Date		Text Description	

Things that you feel are not seen, or not heard	Clues that suggest something is missing	Discussion prompts for group

ARCHIVIST

The **ARCHIVIST's** job is to record conversations of the group during the learning experience and capture discussions by taking notes and minutes during the group's work time. This allows the small group to have a record of what was thought and said. Then, at a later date, the group can refer back to those comments for better understanding of the text. Please be prepared to share your observations with your group.

Ira Glass
Radio Producer, Host, USA,
Born: 1959

"One reason I do the live shows . . . is to remind myself that people hear the show, that it has an audience, that it exists in the world. It's so easy to forget that."

Name	Objective
Date	Text Description

What was said?	Who said it?	Why was it important?

Summary of notes and connections between ideas

Next actions

TECH TIP

Consider using smartphone recording tools like Recorder & SpeakEasy for iPhone or Note Everything for Android if you want to be able to listen more carefully to your conversation. Be sure to ask your group members' permission and record their consent.

Arianna Huffington
Blogger, Journalist, USA, Born: 1950

*"If you take care of your mind,
you take care of the world."*

The **BLOGGER's** job is to write a blog or journal entry from the point of view of a character in the text. What did the character experience, feel, think, or say? What conflicts were they experiencing? What was important to note about the character? What did others say to or about the character? How did the character act? Please be prepared to share your observations with your group.

Name

Objective

Date

Text Description

Name of Blog: www._____

Entry:

TECH TIP

Consider using Edublogs, Bloggger, WordPress, or LiveJournal to set up your own blog.

BODY LINGUIST

Buster Keaton
Actor, Director, Writer,
Producer, USA, 1895–1966

"They say pantomime's a lost art. It's never been a lost art and never will be, because it's too natural to do."

The **BODY LINGUIST's** job is to read movements from the body, face, and gestures. You also need to look at other nonverbal interactions of the characters to discern more about the context of the text. Please be prepared to share your observations with your group.

This list of basic emotions was developed by psychologist Paul Ekman; you might use these as descriptors: anger, amusement, contempt, contentment, embarrassment, excitement, disgust, fear, guilt, happiness, pride in achievement, relief, satisfaction, sensory pleasure, shame, surprise.

Name		Objective	
Date		Text Description	

TECH TIP

Consider using apps designed to help people recognize expressions like Face Apps C, Emotion X, or FaceReader. You might also watch clips online from the John Cleese BBC documentary *Face* to understand the job description more clearly.

Movement, look, gesture, nonverbal interaction	Emotional meaning	Context clues about the movement that help you understand its meaning

CARTOGRAPHER

Paula Scher
Graphic Designer, Painter,
Art Educator, USA, Born 1948

"I began painting maps to invent my own complicated narrative about the way I see and feel about the world."

The **CARTOGRAPHER's** job is to map a text. Keep in mind that you can map space, place, ideas, and even emotions. You may have heard of the concept of making "mind maps," but you can also map places based on other things, like the famous political maps we see during elections in the United States labeling states "red" or "blue."

Please use the space below to creatively map the text you explored. Be prepared to share your findings with your group.

Name	Objective
Date	Text Description

RESOURCES & TECH TIPS

Google Lit Trips (googlelittrips.com) has models of literal maps of narratives

The National Education Association's "Teaching with Maps" page

For less literal ideas about how to map, see "Creative Cartography: 7 Must-Read Books on Maps" at the Brain Pickings site brainpickings.org/2011/01/07/must-read-map-books

CARTOONIST

Charles M. Schulz
Cartoonist (*Peanuts*), USA, 1922–2000

"If you're going to draw a comic strip every day, you're going to have to draw on every experience in your life."

The **CARTOONIST's** job is to draw a six-cell cartoon in the space provided below about something that you found memorable or meaningful from the text, or you can create a sequence that captures "the big picture." Feel free to use stick figures. Captions are also an important aspect of your cartoon. Please be prepared to share your connections with your group.

Below your cartoon please explain in two to four sentences WHY the scene you drew is important.

Name		Objective
Date		Text Description

DRAWING TIP

To make your cartoon more professional, use pencil first and then go over the pencil with a fine-line felt-tip pen. The result is always better and more impressive.

TECH TIP

If you need more cells, consider using word processing software like Microsoft Word or Google Docs to create a table with as many cells as you need to tell your story. Or, use online cartoon creation tools like www.makebeliefscomix.com, www.bitstrips.com, or www.toondoo.com to assist in the creation of your story. If you use any of these options, please attach the artwork to this page.

Why is this drawing important?

CASTING DIRECTOR

The **CASTING DIRECTOR's** job is to critically analyze characters from the text and describe them using the criteria below. Remember, there are "characters" in fiction and nonfiction texts. It is also worth noting that sometimes a place or object can have traits or are personified in a way that makes them function like a character in a story. Please be prepared to share your reactions with your group.

Name

Date

Objective

Text Description

Character Name	Sketch of Character (Headshot)	Physical Description	Important Actions	Important Dialogue	Others' Reaction to the Character	Your Reaction to the Character

CLIMATE & CULTURE ANALYST

Margaret Mead
Cultural Anthropologist, Writer,
USA, 1901–1978

"Our humanity rests upon a series of learned behaviors, woven together into patterns that are infinitely fragile and never directly inherited."

The **CLIMATE & CULTURE ANALYST's** job is to focus on the effect of climate on the culture of an area or region of the world. Climate variables include weather patterns like temperature, precipitation, and wind as well as physical (aka terrestrial) features like mountains, lakes, and vegetation that are linked with the region's climate. Use this LEO to reflect on the impact of cultural characteristics—like work, home, education, food, water, sports, power supplies, education—as they relate to climate. If you are interested in learning more about your region, utilize the Internet for additional information. Please be prepared to share your ideas and hypotheses with your group.

Name	Objective
Date	Text Description

Please place a dot on the location of your climate story:

Climate Variable Observed in This Text	"Normal" Climate Condition for This Area	Noticeable Change (Δ) in Climate Condition Observed in This Text	The Climate Change's (Δ's) Impact on Culture
☐ Average Temp _____ ☐ Wind ☐ Aquatic ☐ Terrestrial ☐ Other			
☐ Average Temp _____ ☐ Wind ☐ Aquatic ☐ Terrestrial ☐ Other			
☐ Average Temp _____ ☐ Wind ☐ Aquatic ☐ Terrestrial ☐ Other			

Mark Zuckerberg
Programmer, Entrepreneur,
USA, Born: 1984

"The thing that we are trying to do at Facebook, is just help people connect and communicate more efficiently."

TECH TIP

Also consider using online tools like Webspiration, Bubbl.us, Gliffy, or Spicynodes.

The **CONNECTOR's** job is to relate your text to other things you have studied in school, your own personal experience, as well as things outside of school (self, text, world). Make sure you are specific—for example, if you are using a passage from a text, write out the EXACT QUOTE OR PASSAGE in the upper boxes with quotation marks. Please be prepared to share your connections with your group.

Name	Objective
Date	Text Description

1. Text selection/quote/detail	Text selection/quote/detail
Reason for Connection	

2. Text selection/quote/detail	Text selection/quote/detail
Reason for Connection	

3. Text selection/quote/detail	Text selection/quote/detail
Reason for Connection	

CRYPTOGRAPHER

Alan Turing
Computer Scientist, Mathematician, Cryptanalyst, UK, 1912–1954

"Machines take me by surprise with great frequency."

The **CRYPTOGRAPHER's** job is to look for (or create) patterns or codes to explain your text. If you are looking at a text like a pop song, you might explain a pattern you see or hear a "verse, chorus, bridge." If you are looking at a landscape, you might reflect on the use of plants, pavement, or open space, if you're looking at a fiction or non-fiction narrative, you might look for codes or patterns of behavior. For math or science texts you might be looking for codes or patterns in data.

Use this LEO to reflect on the patterns you've found in the text. Please be prepared to share your ideas with your group.

Name		Objective	

Date		Text Description	

Observed Data (Can be numbers, images, behavior, etc.)	Suspected Pattern (Can be written as an equation if possible)	Explanation of Pattern

Jon Stewart
Satirist, Writer, TV Host, Producer,
USA, Born: 1962

"If we amplify everything we hear nothing."

DATA ANALYST

Name

Date

Objective

Text Description

The **DATA ANALYST's** job is to review numeric items (quantitative data) presented in the text. Graphs, statistics, measurements, percentages, and other numbers should be your focus. You want to think about how these quantitative measures help us understand the text as well as how they might limit our understandings. Please be prepared to share your connections with your group.

RESOURCE & TECH TIP

To think about what quantitative data might *not* tell us, see this famous *Daily Show* clip about Congressman Paul Ryan's debt plan in 2011: thedailyshow.cc.com/videos/91d8kq/ryan-s-private-savings-republican-deficit-plan. (Note: some of the clip's content is PG-13)

Type of Quantitative Data (check one)	Actual Data	Significance (How this helps understand text)	What This Information Does Not Show Us (How these numbers might be incomplete or misleading)
☐ Graph ☐ Measurement ☐ Number ☐ Percentage ☐ Statistic ☐ Other			
☐ Graph ☐ Measurement ☐ Number ☐ Percentage ☐ Statistic ☐ Other			
☐ Graph ☐ Measurement ☐ Number ☐ Percentage ☐ Statistic ☐ Other			
☐ Graph ☐ Measurement ☐ Number ☐ Percentage ☐ Statistic ☐ Other			
☐ Graph ☐ Measurement ☐ Number ☐ Percentage ☐ Statistic ☐ Other			

DEMOGRAPHER

The **DEMOGRAPHER's** job is to think about the audience the text was designed to appeal to. Things like vocabulary, choice of music, and type of characters often speak to a group of people known in the business world as a "demographic." Please be prepared to share your observations with your group.

TECH TIP

To learn more about demographics, see the PBS documentaries *Merchants of Cool* from *Frontline* or NOVA's *World in the Balance* (available online and on DVD).

Berry Gordy Jr.
Businessman, Founder of Motown Records, USA, Born: 1929

"We released some of our early albums without showing the artists' faces on them. The Marvelettes' album 'Please Mr. Postman' had a picture of a mail box on it; 'Bye Bye Baby' by Mary Wells, a love letter. This practice became less necessary as our music's popularity started overcoming the prejudices."

Name	Objective
Date	Text Description

Focus (check one)	Who Is the Demographic (Audience) for This Text?	Details in the Text That Gave You Clues About Demographic or Audience
☐ Age ☐ Gender ☐ Geography ☐ Lifestyle/Taste ☐ Race ☐ Socioeconomic Status ☐ Other		
☐ Age ☐ Gender ☐ Geography ☐ Lifestyle/Taste ☐ Race ☐ Socioeconomic Status ☐ Other		
☐ Age ☐ Gender ☐ Geography ☐ Lifestyle/Taste ☐ Race ☐ Socioeconomic Status ☐ Other		
☐ Age ☐ Gender ☐ Geography ☐ Lifestyle/Taste ☐ Race ☐ Socioeconomic Status ☐ Other		
☐ Age ☐ Gender ☐ Geography ☐ Lifestyle/Taste ☐ Race ☐ Socioeconomic Status ☐ Other		

DESIGNER

The **DESIGNER's** job is to look for shapes, forms, patterns, and structures in a text. Most texts, from the choruses of songs, to the commercial breaks in television shows, to font choices, to the arrangement of shapes and objects in a painting usually have an underlying design and structure. Please be prepared to share your connections with your group.

Name

Objective

Date

Text Description

Pattern (check one)	Description	Where This Occurs	Importance of This Design
☐ Color ☐ Fonts ☐ Forms ☐ Patterns ☐ Shapes ☐ Structure ☐ Patterns ☐ Texture ☐ Other			
☐ Color ☐ Fonts ☐ Forms ☐ Patterns ☐ Shapes ☐ Structure ☐ Patterns ☐ Texture ☐ Other			
☐ Color ☐ Fonts ☐ Forms ☐ Patterns ☐ Shapes ☐ Structure ☐ Patterns ☐ Texture ☐ Other			
☐ Color ☐ Fonts ☐ Forms ☐ Patterns ☐ Shapes ☐ Structure ☐ Patterns ☐ Texture ☐ Other			

DETECTIVE

Edward R. Murrow
Broadcast Journalist, USA, 1908–1965

"The obscure we see eventually. The completely obvious, it seems, takes longer."

The **DETECTIVE's** job is look at causes and effects. Using the table below, note various events from the text and deduce their causes and effects. Please be prepared to share your analysis with your group.

Name	Objective
Date	Text Description

Causes	Effects

William Goldman
Author, Screenwriter, USA, Born: 1931

"Subtext . . . is not stated in the words, but it is the pulse beating beneath those words; it is the unexpressed subconscious life that brings size and weight to your writing."

DIALOGUE MASTER

The **DIALOGUE MASTER's** job is to focus on a few special spoken sections of the text that you think would be an interesting starting point for discussion. Your focus should make the group aware of the most interesting, puzzling, funny, memorable, or important spoken parts of the text. Please be prepared to share your choices with your group.

TECH TIP

If this is a text that has a time counter, consider finding the time of your scene and recording it below.

Name

Date

Objective

Text Description

Dialogue Description	Reason You Chose Dialogue/Words	Questions for Discussion
Time Counter (if applicable):		
Time Counter (if applicable):		
Time Counter (if applicable):		

ECOLOGIST

The **ECOLOGIST's** job is to explore relationships between biotic (living) and abiotic (nonliving) things and systems. An ecologist looks at a specific ecosystem (like a rainforest or prairie ecosystem) with a scientific goal of exploring the relationships in that system. Ecosystem is also a term used for human systems like computing ecosystems, media ecosystems, educational ecosystems, political ecosystems. Use the LEO to think about your text's "ecosystem" and the relationships in it.

Rachel Carson
Author, Marine Biologist, Conservationist, USA, 1907–1964

"The more clearly we can focus our attention on the wonders and realities of the universe about us, the less taste we shall have for destruction."

RESOURCE

For an interesting look at how a city can be perceived as an ecosystem, see "The City Is an Ecosystem, Pipes and All" by Courtney Humphries at the *Boston Globe* online at goo.gl/9giek5.

Name	Objective
Date	Text Description

Ecosystem Element	Type of Element	Description of Relationship	+ or – for Environment aka Cost/Benefit Analysis
1A	☐ BIOTIC ☐ ABIOTIC		
1B	☐ BIOTIC ☐ ABIOTIC		
2A	☐ BIOTIC ☐ ABIOTIC		
2B	☐ BIOTIC ☐ ABIOTIC		
3A	☐ BIOTIC ☐ ABIOTIC		
3B	☐ BIOTIC ☐ ABIOTIC		
4A	☐ BIOTIC ☐ ABIOTIC		
4B	☐ BIOTIC ☐ ABIOTIC		
4C	☐ BIOTIC ☐ ABIOTIC		

Tyler Perry
Founder of Tyler Perry
Studios, USA, Born: 1969

"I've never chased money. It's always been about what can I do to motivate and inspire people."

The **ECONOMIST's** job is to look at the cost of things and the impact of money on characters in the text. You might hear, read, or see something about a salary, or the cost of a newspaper or food. Also, think broadly about how money affects people's actions and behaviors: Do people with more money communicate differently than people with less money? Does one character have to leave home in order to find work? Make at least 5 observations below. Please be prepared to share your observations with your group.

Name

Objective

Date

Text Description

My observations regarding the cost of things and the effect of money on people's behaviors and actions in the text are as follows:

1.

2.

3.

4.

5.

FACT CHECKER

The **FACT CHECKER's** job is use the library or Internet to corroborate the data presented in your text. Whether your text is fiction (made-up) or nonfiction (real) there are often numbers or events that may be presented as reality when in fact they are partially true, a stretch of the truth, a misleading statement, or an outright fabrication. In the space below list four facts from the text (they can be numbers, data, events, etc.) and decide how reliable they may be.

Katharine Graham
Writer, Publisher of *The Washington Post*, USA, 1917–2001

"If we had failed to pursue the facts as far as they led, we would have denied the public any knowledge of an unprecedented scheme of political surveillance and sabotage."

TECH TIP

Consider using online tools like snopes.com to research urban legends, factcheck.org for political material, or use the reference links on Wikipedia pages to corroborate facts on more general topics.

Name	Objective
Date	Text Description

Event/Fact Presented	Location in Text	True or False	Research to Support or Refute Fact

Vera Wang
Fashion Designer, USA, Born: 1978

"I dress the individualist, the one that comprehends fashion."

FASHION CRITIC

The **FASHION CRITIC's** job is to comment on how the characters appear in the text. Hairstyles, clothes, and styles should be noted. If it is an audio text, there may be notable details about fashion. Please be prepared to share your thoughts with your group.

Name	Objective
Date	Text Description

Fashion Observation	Details You Noticed	Questions and Opinions About the Style/Fashion

FRAMER

Diane Arbus
Photographer, USA, 1923–1971

"Lately I've been struck with how I really love what you can't see in a photograph."

The **FRAMER's** job is to think about what is included in the text, as well as what is excluded. Every text, whether print, audio, or visual, gives you a point of view that focuses on certain things and ignores others. In the space below draw or write the things you think are IN the text and make guesses about information that might have been left out of the text.

Please be prepared to share your observations with your group.

Name	Objective

Date	Text Description

Things That Might Have Been Left Out/Excluded:

Things That Were Focused On/Included:

Will Wright

Game Designer, Entrepreneur, USA,
Born: 1960

"I think the idea of having a game based on reality is compelling right off the bat because everyone has some experience with the subject of the game."

GAMER

The **GAMER's** job is to imagine the text as a board game or video game. Many games tend to be built around rules, roles, structures, and rewards. In the space below draw a board game or draw screen shots of the text as a video game. Think carefully about conflicts, rewards, and "if-then" statements. For example: "IF I ditch class, THEN I will get a detention." These inputs (IF) and outputs (THEN) drive many games. Please be prepared to share your thoughts with your group.

Name	Objective

Date	Text Description

RESOURCE

Consider watching Jane McGonigal's TED Talk, "Gaming Can Make a Better World" (goo.gl/aZt2) to see how reality and games collide.

GENEALOGIST

Henry Louis Gates Jr.
Author, Documentary Filmmaker, Essayist, Professor, USA, Born: 1950

The **GENEALOGIST's** job is to visually capture the relationships between people. They may be familial relationships (mother, father, son, daughter, etc.) or they may be other ways people are connected (boss/employee, friend/enemy, teacher/student, etc.) You may draw this as a tree (where the root is the most important person or idea) or a more traditional flow chart. For more creative ways people and ideas can be connected, do a Google image search for "Rock & Roll family tree" or "Art movements as a family tree." Please be prepared to share your observations with your group.

"If you share a common ancestor with somebody, you're related to them. It doesn't mean that you're going to invite them to the family reunion, but it means that you share DNA. I think it's fascinating."

Name		Objective

Date		Text Description

RESOURCE

For help making the tree consider using WikiTree.com or WeRelate.org.

GENRE GURU

"Perhaps it sounds ridiculous, but the best thing that young filmmakers should do is to get hold of a camera and some film and make a movie of any kind at all."

The **GENRE GURU's** job is to look for traits that categorize the text. First, is the text fiction or nonfiction? How do you know? What support do you have to verify your response? From there, what type of fiction or nonfiction is the text? How do you know? Be specific in your comments.

Please be prepared to share your observations with your group.

Name	Objective
Date	Text Description

There are many genres of texts, including familiar categories like **science fiction**, **romance**, **documentary**, **comedy**, or **horror**. If you're looking at a more journalistic text, it could be **investigative reporting**, **news magazine**, or **memoir**. If you're looking at visual arts, a medium (**photography**, **oil painting**, **sculpture**, or **collage**) is often considered a genre and may even be categorized as a subgenre like **expressionism**, **pop art**, **folk art**, **landscape**, etc. Music texts come in familiar genres like **jazz**, **rock**, **pop**, **country**, **hip-hop**, and **classical**. No matter what text you have, think about how you might categorize it and why you would classify it that way.

Genre	Traits of the Text That Support My Choice
☐ Fiction ☐ Nonfiction	
Subgenre	

GEOGRAPHER

Jehane Noujaim
Documentarian, Pangaea Day Film Fest Creator, USA, Born: 1974

"Imagine if you could get the world's filmmakers, known and unknown, to get together [and make] a story for the world, by the world."

The **GEOGRAPHER's** job is to record and track the geographic locations in the text. Your text might take place all in one town or all over the world. Some texts might even take place in fictional locations (e.g., Middle Earth from *Lord of the Rings*). Your job is to create a *map* of the locations below. Please be prepared to share your observations with your group.

Name

Date

Objective

Text Description

TECH TIP

Consider using Google Maps, Google Lit Trips, Four Square, or Gowalla to create a geotagged map for existing geographic locations.

Thelma Schoonmaker
Film Editor, USA, Born: 1940

"You get to contribute so significantly in the editing room because you shape the movie and the performances . . . you give their work rhythm and pace and sometimes adjust the structure to make the film work—to make it start to flow up there on the screen."

The **HIGHLIGHTER's** job is to focus on a few special sections of the text that you think would be a great starting point for discussion. Your focus should make the group aware of the most interesting, puzzling, funny, memorable, or important parts of the text. Please be prepared to share your choices with your group.

TECH TIP

If the text has a time counter, consider finding the time of your scene and recording it below.

Name		Objective	
Date		Text Description	

Scene Description	Reason You Chose Scene/Highlight	Questions for Discussion
Time counter (if applicable):		
Time counter (if applicable):		
Time counter (if applicable):		

IMAGERY HUNTER

Maya Lin
Sculptor, Landscape Artist, USA,
Born: 1959

"I try to give people a different way of looking at their surroundings. That's art to me."

The **IMAGERY HUNTER's** job is to look for images or metaphors that can be linked to a theme, idea, event, person, or cultural value. Remember, a metaphor compares two ideas or objects and does not use "like" or "as," e.g., "the road was a ribbon of moonlight." Visual metaphors mirror their written counterparts, but they are done with images. Please be prepared to share your observations with your group.

Name		Objective

Date		Text Description

Image or Metaphor	Location/Description in Text	Reason This Has Symbolic or Metaphorical Meaning
	Time counter (if applicable):	
	Time counter (if applicable):	
	Time counter (if applicable):	

Edward Tufte

Statistician, Political and Computer Scientist, Professor, USA, Born: 1942

"We shouldn't abbreviate the truth but rather get a new method of presentation."

INFORMATION DESIGNER

The **INFORMATION DESIGNER's** job is to figure out ways to present data. With the advent of powerful computing software, presentations have gone beyond traditional graphs into "infographics." Infographics tell a visual story using data you've found. Infographics are uniquely suited to engage your audience visually with numbers. Use this LEO to reflect on your text through a visual or graph. Please be prepared to share your ideas with your group.

Name	Objective

Date	Text Description

RESOURCES & TECH TIPS

The infographic collection at coolinfographics.com

Nicholas Feltron's annual reports, where he charts 365 days of his personal life through data visualization (feltron.com)

GraphJam (at memebase.cheezburger.com)

Jessica Hagy's thisisindexed.com

Infographic creation sites (Easel.ly, Creately, Gliffy, Infogr.am, and Visually)

INTUITOR

Oprah Winfrey
Actor, Talk Show Host,
Entrepreneur, USA, Born: 1954

*"Allowing the truth of who you are—
your spiritual self—to rule your life
means you stop the struggle and learn
to move with the flow of your life."*

The **INTUITOR's** job is to look for parts of the text that create feelings or predictions about the future. In some ways, this person is like a therapist (trying to interpret or understand people's emotions); in other ways, this person is like a fortune-teller trying to foresee or intuit what lies ahead. Please be prepared to share your observations with your group.

Name		Objective
Date		Text Description

This list of basic emotions was developed by psychologist Paul Ekman; you might use these as descriptors: anger, amusement, contempt, contentment, embarrassment, excitement, disgust, fear, guilt, happiness, pride in achievement, relief, satisfaction, sensory pleasure, shame, surprise.

Scene Description	Feeling/Prediction	Reason You Are Connecting Idea to the Text (or, Why Does it Make You Feel That Way?)
Time counter (if applicable):		
Time counter (if applicable):		
Time counter (if applicable):		

LAWYER

The **LAWYER's** job is to create a case with support and evidence for a person, situation, or idea. Remember, good lawyers also consider the other side of the case and will use the opposition's arguments to prove *their* point.

Please be prepared to share your ideas with your group.

Name	Objective
Date	Text Description

Conflict	Your Case or Support for How to Resolve That Conflict	The Other Side's Case or a Detail That Supports Their Argument	At Least 3 Details Supporting Your Case/Argument

METAPHOR MAKER

Sandra Cisneros
Poet, Writer, USA,
Born: 1954

"Writing is like sewing together what I call these 'buttons,' these bits and pieces."

The **METAPHOR MAKER's** job is to create a metaphor for the text you explored. This means taking two unrelated objects to make connections among characters, data, events, or ideas, to give your group unique insights into a text. You can do this by writing your own metaphors or by drawing/visualizing a metaphor for your text. Some famous metaphoric language includes "the apple of my eye," "busy as a bee," she had a "heart of gold." Please be prepared to share your ideas with your group.

Name	Objective
Date	Text Description

This Element in Text (draw or describe a person, object, event, setting, idea, etc.)	Is Like/Can Be Compared to (draw or describe a new unique person, object, event, setting, idea, etc.)	Because . . .

Barbara Walters
Journalist, Talk Show Host,
USA, Born: 1929

"Wait for those unguarded moments. Relax the mood and, like the child dropping off to sleep, the subject often reveals his [sic] truest self."

MOOD CATCHER

The **MOOD CATCHER's** job is to describe the mood and tone of the text. Use adjectives—perhaps from the bank below—to capture the tone and mood. Be sure to support your descriptions with evidence and details from the text. Please be prepared to share your ideas with your group.

Name		Objective	
Date		Text Description	

Some sample adjectives that might describe mood or tone:

angelic, ashamed, blaring, blissful, bitter, carefree, cheerful, clear, distain, drab, ebullient, elated, evil, excited, fanciful, formal, frightened, funny, gloomy, happy, hopeful, hopeless, ironic, jolly, lonely, matter-of-fact, muffled, mysterious, optimistic, pessimistic, playful, pompous, romantic, sad, scared, sentimental, sophisticated, sour, taciturn, thunderous, witty, zany

Focus	Descriptive Word	Details Supporting Your Choice
Mood The feeling the reader/viewer/listener gets from interacting with the text		
Tone Our best guess at the author's feelings and attitude toward the text; the way the author's feelings are expressed through setting, colors, vocabulary, and other details		

NUMERIST

The **NUMERIST's** job is to listen for language that can be translated to mathematical operations or numerical investigations. See morenewmath .com for humorous ways everyday events can be turned into equations.

Use this LEO to highlight scenarios that can be translated into math or equations. Please be prepared to share your ideas and hypotheses with your group.

Shakuntala Devi
Writer, Mental Calculator,
India, 1929–2013

"Without mathematics, there's nothing you can do. Everything around you is mathematics. Everything around you is numbers."

Name	Objective

Date	Text Description

Operation **MULTIPLY** (at this rate, factor of, multiplied by, product of, times, doubled, tripled) Scenario this applies to in text:	Operation **ADDITION** (added to, additionally, another, altogether, combined, increased by, more than, in all, in all body, together, total, words ending in "er" like higher faster, larger, etc.) Scenario this applies to in text:
Operation **DIVISION** (each, equally, per separate, quotient, ratio of) Scenario this applies to in text:	Operation **SUBTRACTION** (decreased by, difference between or of, minus, fewer than, how many more left, more than/less than, remaining) Scenario this applies to in text:

Kathy Bates
Actor, Director, USA,
Born: 1948

"I try to always stretch myself to fit the characters that have been presented."

The **PERFORMER's** job is to do some type of performance of your text for the group. You might interpret what you observed by acting, create a tiny skit where you play multiple roles, do a news report, or even stage a tableau (this is when you make "frozen" poses to capture a moment—think the famous painting of George Washington crossing the Delaware River or playing Charades) for the members in your group.

Use the space below to draw the tableau(s) you might share with your group or some notes to guide your performance.

Name	Objective
Date	Text Description

PLOT MASTER

Tina Fey
Actor, Comedian, Writer, Producer, USA, Born: 1970

The **PLOT MASTER's** job is to fill in a plot chart with the introduction, rising action, conflict, climax, falling action, and the conclusion. Note that there may be more than one plotline in the text. Please be prepared to share your diagram(s) with your group.

"Don't be too precious or attached to anything you write. Let things be malleable."

Name	Objective

Date	Text Description

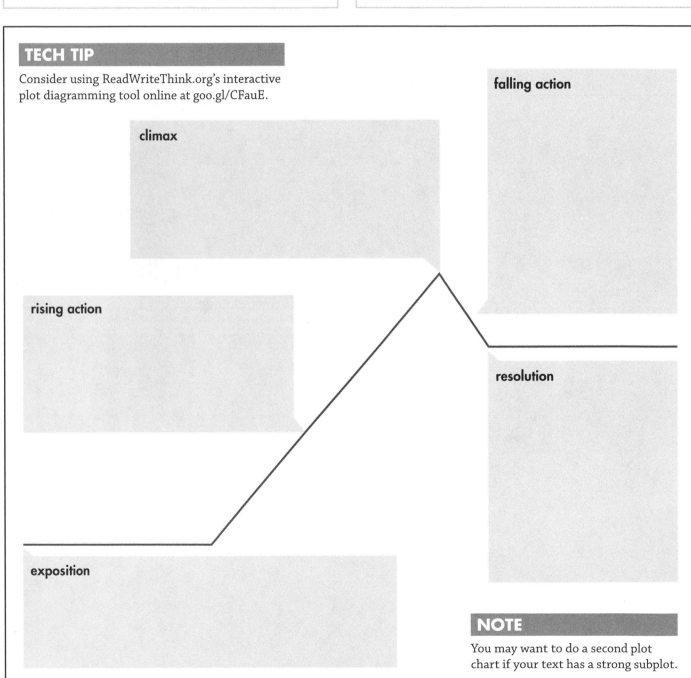

TECH TIP

Consider using ReadWriteThink.org's interactive plot diagramming tool online at goo.gl/CFauE.

falling action

climax

rising action

resolution

exposition

NOTE

You may want to do a second plot chart if your text has a strong subplot.

Bob Dylan
Author, Singer-Songwriter,
USA, Born: 1941

"This land is your land and this land is my land, sure, but the world is run by those that never listen to music anyway."

POET

The **POET's** job is to summarize, interpret, and/or comment on the text using poetry or lyrics. Of course, poems and lyrics don't always have to rhyme (this is called free verse), but rhyming is always fun. Unlike prose, in poetry you do not have to follow the rules or conventions of grammar, so be creative. Please be prepared to share your poems/lyrics with your group.

Name

Objective

Date

Text Description

Title of Poem/Song:
By:

Lines

TECH TIP

Consider using online rhyming dictionaries or an application like Rhyme Genie to help you create rhymes.

PREDICTOR

Fareed Zakaria
Journalist, Author, USA, Born: 1964

The **PREDICTOR's** job is to try to figure out what might happen next in the text. How do you know? What support and reasons can you use to back up or support your prediction? Please be prepared to share your choices with your group.

"I think what happened is we've realized the path to modernity is actually a very complicated one with many roads or byways or lanes and countries travel all along it."

Name	Objective

Date	Text Description

Description of Scene (That Gives You a Clue About What Might Happen)	Reason You Chose This Part of the Text	Questions for Discussion
Time counter (if applicable):		
Time counter (if applicable):		
Time counter (if applicable):		

George Lucas
Writer, Director, Producer, Founder of
Lucasfilm, USA, Born: 1944

"You have to find something that you love enough to be able to take risks, jump over the hurdles and break through the brick walls that are always going to be placed in front of you. If you don't have that kind of feeling for what it is you are doing, you'll stop at the first giant hurdle."

The **PRODUCER's** job is to help group members stay focused and on task, take notes, and stay within the time limits of the assigned task. The Producer is also available to help other group members with their assigned task if they need assistance or motivation. If a group member is off task, the Producer will remind that member of his or her job/role. At the end of the work session, the Producer will collect the entire team's work and collect the evaluation sheets from all the group members to hand in to the teacher. Please be prepared to share observations about your group.

Name	Objective
Date	Text Description

Today I had the following positive interactions with group members:

1.

2.

3.

4.

5.

6.

7.

RHETORICIAN

James Baldwin
Novelist, Essayist, Playwright, Poet, Social Critic, USA, 1924–1987

The **RHETORICIAN's** job is to consider the type of appeals used in a text to persuade its reader. Aristotle believed that the most effective arguments contained all three appeals: ethos (the credibility of the writer), logos (how well logic is used), and pathos (emotional appeals to a specific audience).

"The paradox of education is precisely this—that as one begins to become conscious, one begins to examine the society in which he is being educated."

Use this LEO to reflect on the use of ethos, logos, and pathos in your text. Please be prepared to share your ideas and hypotheses with your group.

Name	Objective
Date	Text Description

LOGOS
(Reason/Logic)

ETHOS
(Credibility/Author/Institution)

PATHOS
(Values/Beliefs/Audience/Emotion)

Patti Smith

Singer-Songwriter, Poet,
Visual Artist, USA, Born: 1946

"When I was younger, I felt it was my duty to wake people up. I thought poetry was asleep. I thought rock 'n' roll was asleep."

The **SENSOR's** job is to focus on the way that the colors, textures, lighting, and lines of the text present themselves. While this will most often apply to visual texts, many types of media have textures. For example, the sounds of an electric guitar can create a different texture than that of an acoustic guitar—the former is often loud and bombastic, while the latter is usually organic or peaceful. When you look at a text, what do you notice about the textures? Do they help create a certain feeling or emotion? Please be prepared to share your observations with your group.

Name		Objective	
Date		Text Description	

Some sample adjectives you might use: abstract, angular, bold, bumpy, complex, curved, dark, dotted, dramatic, dull, earthy, flat, geometric, high/low angle, light, loose, natural, open, organic, pale, scratchy, short, sketchy, skinny, smooth, soft, solid, straight, strong, ugly, vibrant, violent, wide

Focus (check one)	Description of What You Noticed and Where in the Text	Adjective Describing What You Sensed from This Element and Why
☐ Line ☐ Color ☐ Framing ☐ Space ☐ Texture ☐ Lighting ☐ Shadow ☐ Sounds ☐ Other		
☐ Line ☐ Color ☐ Framing ☐ Space ☐ Texture ☐ Lighting ☐ Shadow ☐ Sounds ☐ Other		
☐ Line ☐ Color ☐ Framing ☐ Space ☐ Texture ☐ Lighting ☐ Shadow ☐ Sounds ☐ Other		
☐ Line ☐ Color ☐ Framing ☐ Space ☐ Texture ☐ Lighting ☐ Shadow ☐ Sounds ☐ Other		

SET DESIGNER

Julie Taymor
Director of Theatre, Film, Opera, USA, Born: 1952

"I think we all see the world from our own little unique bubble."

The **SET DESIGNER's** job is to carefully sketch the details of at least one interior and/or exterior location related to the text. Please be prepared to share your "set designs" with your group.

Name		Objective	

Date		Text Description	

TECH TIP

Consider using www.floorplanner.com, www.3dream.net, Google SketchUp, or Second Life to recreate the settings from your text.

Martin Scorsese
Writer, Director, Film Historian,
Producer, USA, Born: 1942

"Now more than ever we need to talk to each other, to listen to each other and understand how we see the world, and cinema is the best medium for doing this."

The **SOCIOLOGIST's** job is to look at the culture, customs, and social norms portrayed in the text. Look carefully at how women, men, and children, races or classes of people interact with each other. What are their roles in society and what is expected of these different types of people? Additionally, what behaviors and customs seem unique, foreign, or different from what you normally see? What types of things seem off-limits or "taboo" to characters in the text? Please record your observations in the graphic organizer below and share your comments with your group.

Name

Objective

Date

Text Description

Focus (check one)	Details You Saw/Noticed About the Cultures, Customs, and Social Norms	Questions and Thoughts About the Cultures, Customs, and Social Norms
☐ Women ☐ Men ☐ Children ☐ Customs ☐ Race ☐ Socioeconomic Status ☐ Other		
☐ Women ☐ Men ☐ Children ☐ Customs ☐ Race ☐ Socioeconomic Status ☐ Other		
☐ Women ☐ Men ☐ Children ☐ Customs ☐ Race ☐ Socioeconomic Status ☐ Other		
☐ Women ☐ Men ☐ Children ☐ Customs ☐ Race ☐ Socioeconomic Status ☐ Other		
☐ Women ☐ Men ☐ Children ☐ Customs ☐ Race ☐ Socioeconomic Status ☐ Other		

SOUND MIXER

The **SOUND MIXER's** job is to listen for music and sound effects (they can be fake sounds like those of a laser gun, or sounds related to your location like seagulls near the ocean) in your text. If you have a visual or print text, you can look for things that allow you to imagine sounds and songs in your head. For each sound, please explain where you heard or found it, how it affects you emotionally, and the meaning it adds to the text. Please be prepared to share your ideas and feelings about the sounds with your group.

**J. Dilla
(James Dewitt Yancey)**
Musician, MC, DJ, Producer,
USA, 1974–2006

"When I make my music I want people to feel what I feel, I want people to feel that energy or whatever it was because I make it straight from the heart."

Name	Objective
Date	Text Description

Music/Sound Effect Description and Location	What You Think Created the Sound	Emotional Effect on Text	Impact on Meaning of Text	Your Reaction
Time counter (if applicable):				
Time counter (if applicable):				
Time counter (if applicable):				
Time counter (if applicable):				

SOUNDTRACK SUPERVISOR

John Williams
Composer, Pianist, Conductor,
USA, Born: 1932

"So much of what we do is ephemeral and quickly forgotten, even by ourselves, so it's gratifying to have something you have done linger in people's memories."

Name

Date

Objective

Text Description

The **SOUNDTRACK SUPERVISOR's** job is to listen (or sometimes read and look) for music in the text. Once you have identified a song or soundtrack, please fill in the details about the song below. Note that the term *instrumentation* below asks you to listen for the types of instruments used. Does the song have traditional rock instruments like guitar and drums or orchestral instruments like strings, pianos, and horns? You can also create a playlist if no soundtrack exists.

TECH TIP

Consider using the smartphone app Shazam (www.shazam.com) to identify songs. Also, if you want to learn more about the song's composer, consider using the All Music reference site to learn more (allmusic.com).

Music/Song Description Location in Text	Genre	Title & Artist (if known)	Instrumentation	Emotional Effect on Text	Impact on Meaning of Text	Your Reaction
Time counter (if applicable):	☐ Classical ☐ Country ☐ Electronic ☐ Hip-Hop ☐ Jazz ☐ Rock ☐ World ☐ Other					
Time counter (if applicable):	☐ Classical ☐ Country ☐ Electronic ☐ Hip-Hop ☐ Jazz ☐ Rock ☐ World ☐ Other					
Time counter (if applicable):	☐ Classical ☐ Country ☐ Electronic ☐ Hip-Hop ☐ Jazz ☐ Rock ☐ World ☐ Other					
Time counter (if applicable):	☐ Classical ☐ Country ☐ Electronic ☐ Hip-Hop ☐ Jazz ☐ Rock ☐ World ☐ Other					

SUMMARIZER

Diane Sawyer
Television Journalist, USA, Born: 1945

The **SUMMARIZER's** job is to briefly summarize the work the group has done today or the main ideas from today's texts. List the key points of today's work and then list the essence or main ideas of each key point.

Please be prepared to share your observations with your group.

"Every time somebody tries to go in and reinvent what we do, it always ends up being more about technology and sets, and flash and dash, forgetting the main thing, which is interesting people saying interesting, important things."

Name	Objective

Date	Text Description

Summary of today's reading/work:

Key points, events, or ideas:

1.

2.

3.

4.

5.

6.

7.

8.

TECH SPECIALIST

The **TECH SPECIALIST's** job is to look at the *use* of technology in the text (e.g., how the film is shot or a song's use of sound effects) and/or the depiction of technology in the text (methods of transportation, communication, appliances, etc.). You might talk about the technological differences between the time period in the text and the present day or the technologies used to create the text. Please be prepared to share your observations with your group.

Name

Objective

Date

Text Description

Technology in Text	Details of What You Saw/Noticed	Questions and Thoughts About What You Saw/Noticed

TIME CATCHER

Octavia E. Butler
Novelist, USA, 1947–2006

"People who think about time travel stories sometimes think that going back in time would be fun because you would have all the information you needed to be much more astute than the people there, when the truth is of course you wouldn't."

The **TIME CATCHER's** job is to carefully look at the language, technology, descriptions, and objects (aka context clues) that create the space, place, and time of a text. In other words, the Time Catcher uses context clues to figure out the setting (time and place) of a text. Please be prepared to share your observations with your group.

Name	Objective
Date	Text Description

In the space below list 8 clues that allowed you to figure out the time period of the piece you're reading/listening to/viewing.

Context Clue	Information This Gives Us About the Setting

Ken Burns
Director and Producer of Documentaries,
USA, Born: 1953

"History is malleable. A new cache of diaries can shed new light, and archaeological evidence can challenge our popular assumptions."

The **TIMELINER's** job is to create chronologies for people, events, or ideas in your text. If you have a still image (photo or work of art), you might imagine what happens before and after the image you are focusing on. You may even decide to create multiple or parallel timelines for your text. Be creative and please be prepared to share your observations with your group.

Name

Date

Objective

Text Description

TECH TIP

Consider using online tools like timetoast.com, timeliner.com, timerime.com or preceden.com to create your timeline digitally.

NOTE TO STUDENTS

You do not need to use the straight, linear timeline pictured here—if you want to create a more dynamic, sloping, curving, spiral, or jagged timeline, feel free to create your unique visualization of time on the back of the page.

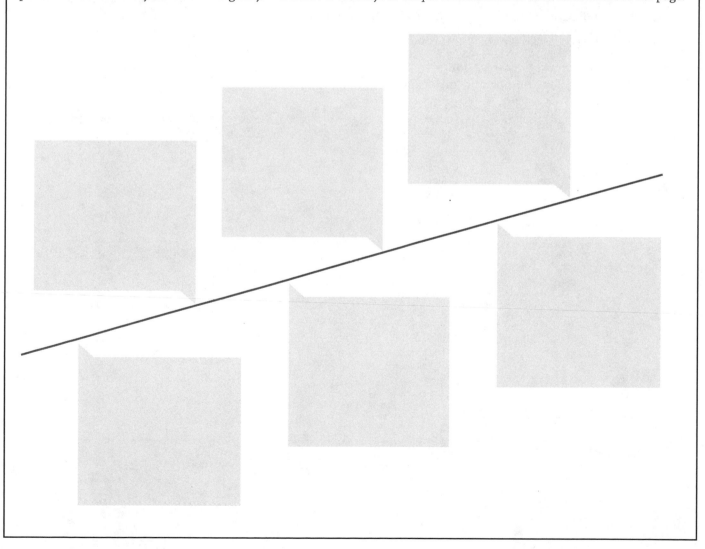

TRUTHINESS DETECTOR

Stephen Colbert
Writer, Television Host, Actor, Comedian, USA
Born: 1964

The **TRUTHINESS DETECTOR's** job is to look for ideas or statements in the text that can be interpreted as fact, opinion, assumption, or bias.

Use this LEO to reflect on facts, opinions, and bias in your text. Please be prepared to share your ideas and hypotheses with your group

"Truthiness is tearing apart our country, and I don't mean the argument over who came up with the word. I don't know whether it's a new thing, but it's certainly a current thing, in that it doesn't seem to matter what facts are. It used to be, everyone was entitled to their own opinion, but not their own facts. But that's not the case anymore. Facts matter not at all. Perception is everything."

| Name | | Objective | |

| Date | | Text Description | |

Facts are objective, which means they are provable, measurable, observable, and verifiable.

Opinions are subjective judgments that require evidence to be considered valid. For example, people can have different viewpoints about a movie, band, or TV show using shared criteria.

Assumptions are based on patterns and things believed to be true.

Bias shows a preference or perception for an idea, group of people, set of values, or attitudes. These can be irrational, based on fear, humor, and/or misinformation.

Idea/Statement Presented	Fact, Opinion, or Bias	Reason/Research to Support Whether Idea Is Fact, Opinion, or Bias
	☐ Fact ☐ Opinion ☐ Bias ☐ Assumption	
	☐ Fact ☐ Opinion ☐ Bias ☐ Assumption	
	☐ Fact ☐ Opinion ☐ Bias ☐ Assumption	
	☐ Fact ☐ Opinion ☐ Bias ☐ Assumption	

VISUALIZER

The **VISUALIZER's** job is to draw a scene from the text or to create an image of the text (this can include symbols and logos).

Please be prepared to share your image with your group.

Name

Objective

Date

Text Description

TECH TIP

Consider using Microsoft Paint, Google SketchUp, MugTug's Sketchpad, or an app like Brushes or iDoodle2lite to draw digitally.

WEB MASTER

Larry Page
Computer Scientist, Cofounder & CEO of
Google, USA, Born: 1973

*"Basically, our goal is to organize the world's
information and to make it universally accessible
and useful."*

The **WEB MASTER's** job for this portion of the text is to draw a mind map to show your understanding of the text. Start with what you think is a big or main idea and use shapes to make connections. Please be prepared to share your web with your group.

Name

Date

Objective

Text Description

TECH TIP

You may do this role digitally using Inspiration, Bubbl.us, etc.

Lucille Ball
Comedian, Actor, Model, Executive,
USA, 1911–1989

"The more things you do, the more you can do."

The **WILD CARD's** job is to choose any role that you would like to be, or you can CREATE YOUR OWN ROLE! Just remember to support your work appropriately in the space provided below. Please be prepared to share your work with your group.

Name

Date

Objective

Text Description

TECH TIP

Consider using online software or a website that you enjoy to reflect on the text in your own unique way.

WONDERER

Spike Lee
Director, Writer, Producer, Actor, USA,
Born: 1957

"You've really got to start hitting the books because it's no joke out here."

The **WONDERER's** job is to write down questions about the text. After you share those questions with your group, you might talk about your group's responses or barriers that are preventing the group from finding an answer. Be sure to ask at least 6 questions below. Please be prepared to share your questions with your group.

Name	Objective

Date	Text Description

I wondered about . . . because . . . (give details to support your question).

1.

2.

3.

4.

5.

6.

Nora Ephron
Author, Screenwriter, Director,
Producer, USA, 1941–2012

"Reading is everything. Reading makes me feel like I've accomplished something, learned something, become a better person. Reading makes me smarter. Reading gives me something to talk about later on. Reading is the unbelievably healthy way my attention deficit disorder medicates itself."

The **WORDSMITH's** job is to find words that are important, new, puzzling, unfamiliar, or unusual. Jot down words that sound unusual or unfamiliar and look them up or try to figure out the word's meaning from context clues. Please be prepared to discuss your choices with your group.

TECH TIP

Consider using the Visual Thesaurus (visualthesaurus.com) or Merriam-Webster's Visual Dictionary (visual.merriam-webster.com) to help you visualize the words.

Name		Objective	
Date		Text Description	

Word	Where in This Text Did You Encounter This Word?	Definition or Picture	What Context Clues Support Your Definition?

WORLDVIEWER

Suheir Hammad
Poet, Actor, Author, Political
Activist, USA, Born: 1973

*"I'm just happy to talk to people
about their experience, they don't
need to have the same one I've had."*

The **WORLDVIEWER's** job is to think about the point of view of the characters and/or authors of the texts. Everyone's worldview (way of seeing the world) is unique, and each person or character sees things differently. Who is telling the story? Is there bias that is evident or an opinion from a particular character that is obvious? Also, consider the camera angles or shots of scenes, if appropriate. Words, lyrics, choice of color, or instrument can also "color" a character's worldview as presented by an artist. Please be prepared to share your findings with your group.

Name	Objective
Date	Text Description

Point of View You're Looking at
Author or Character:

How do you know this is a character's point of view?

What makes this point of view unique?

I know because

Is bias evident?

Any audio or visual choices (angles, colors, placement of objects) that let you enter a character's world:

X-CAVATOR

The **X-CAVATOR's** job is to look for the relevant variables (the "x" in X-cavator) in a text. When we talk about things like events and relationships, they can be influenced by a series of variables that determine their outcome. We often read a news article where the focus is on certain variables—if someone is talking about the success of a company, sports team, or public policy, they might talk about the variables that create change.

Use this LEO to reflect on variables in a text. Please be prepared to share your ideas and hypotheses with your group.

Name	Objective

Date	Text Description

A **dependent variable** depends on other variables. Your weight might depend on how much you eat or exercise. An **independent variable** is not changed by other variables. For example, your age will not change based on how much you exercise or eat.

Variable	Variable Type (check one)	Impact/Importance of Variable
	☐ Dependent ☐ Independent	
	☐ Dependent ☐ Independent	
	☐ Dependent ☐ Independent	
	☐ Dependent ☐ Independent	

In the space below explain what are the least and most significant variables. Why?

Explain how all these variables interact and what happens when they are all combined.

INDIVIDUAL/ GROUP EVALUATION

Standards-Based Version I

The **INDIVIDUAL/GROUP EVALUATOR's** job is to evaluate your work as well as the work of every member of the group. This sheet will be handed in at the end of the day/lesson/project for a participation grade. Please hand in one sheet for each day of group work.

Name	Objective
Date	Text Description

Name:		LEO:		
Standard:				
Exceeds Standard	Above Standard	Meets Standard	Meets Standard with Help	Does Not Meet Standard

Name:		LEO:		
Standard:				
Exceeds Standard	Above Standard	Meets Standard	Meets Standard with Help	Does Not Meet Standard

Name:		LEO:		
Standard:				
Exceeds Standard	Above Standard	Meets Standard	Meets Standard with Help	Does Not Meet Standard

Name:		LEO:		
Standard:				
Exceeds Standard	Above Standard	Meets Standard	Meets Standard with Help	Does Not Meet Standard

INDIVIDUAL/ GROUP EVALUATION

Standards-Based Version II

The **INDIVIDUAL/GROUP EVALUATOR's** job is to evaluate your work as well as the work of every member of the group. This sheet will be handed in at the end of the day/lesson/project for a participation grade. Please hand in one sheet for each day of group work.

Name	Objective
Date	Text Description

Name:		LEO:
Standard:		

Innovating	Emerging	Developing

Name:		LEO:
Standard:		

Innovating	Emerging	Developing

Name:		LEO:
Standard:		

Innovating	Emerging	Developing

Name:		LEO:
Standard:		

Innovating	Emerging	Developing

INDIVIDUAL/ GROUP EVALUATION

Daymond John
Entrepreneur, Shark Tank Judge,
Author, Speaker, USA, Born: 1969

"If you want to do something well, you've got to be committed to it. You've got to do it fully."

Point-Based Version

The **INDIVIDUAL/GROUP EVALUATOR's** job is to evaluate your work as well as the work of every member of the group. This sheet will be handed in at the end of the day/lesson/project for a participation grade. Please hand in one sheet for each day of group work.

Name		Objective	
Date		Text Description	

Name:		LEO:		
Standard:				
Exceeds Standard	Above Standard	Meets Standard	Meets Standard with Help	Does Not Meet Standard
Points	Points	Points	Points	Points

Name:		LEO:		
Standard:				
Exceeds Standard	Above Standard	Meets Standard	Meets Standard with Help	Does Not Meet Standard
Points	Points	Points	Points	Points

Name:		LEO:		
Standard:				
Exceeds Standard	Above Standard	Meets Standard	Meets Standard with Help	Does Not Meet Standard
Points	Points	Points	Points	Points

Name:		LEO:		
Standard:				
Exceeds Standard	Above Standard	Meets Standard	Meets Standard with Help	Does Not Meet Standard
Points	Points	Points	Points	Points

Key Terms

21st-CENTURY SKILLS are based on the idea that traditional schooling is designed for the needs of the 19th century. Twenty-first century skills emphasize more interdisciplinary and student-centered classrooms suited to the needs of emerging personal, professional, economic, and technological realities.

ACTIVE LEARNING refers to several models of instruction that shift the responsibility for learning to learners. Active learning immerses students directly and actively in the learning process itself. This means that students are receiving information, participating, doing, and creating things with informed knowledge and understanding instead of simply regurgitating isolated facts and skills.

ASSESSMENT is the use of a variety of procedures to collect information about learning and instruction. Formative and summative assessments are two types of assessment.

> FORMATIVE ASSESSMENT provides immediate feedback to both the teacher and student regarding the learning process. It is an ongoing and daily process.

> SUMMATIVE ASSESSMENT is commonly referred to as assessment of learning, in which the focus is on determining what the student has learned at the end of a unit of instruction or at the end of a grade level (e.g., through grade-level, standardized assessments).

An **AUTHENTIC ASSESSMENT** is a task or project that allows students to share their work with an audience beyond their classroom. School plays and musical performances are common authentic assessments. Science fairs and presentations to school boards, other classes, online galleries, or community organizations are examples of authentic assessments. High-quality authentic assessments are usually driven by a purpose framed by a rubric. Rubrics can be created by students or teachers.

COLLABORATIVE LEARNING is based on the idea that learning is a social act in which the participants talk among themselves. It is through talk, conversation, and discussion that learning occurs. Cooperative learning involves collaboration. Or another way to view this idea is that collaborative learning is necessary for successful cooperative learning.

COOPERATIVE LEARNING is a successful teaching strategy in which small teams, each with students of different levels of ability, use a variety of learning activities to improve their understanding of a subject. Usually more teacher centered than collaborative learning, very clear structures guide students to clear goals. Each member of a team is responsible not only for learning what is taught but also for helping teammates learn, thus each individual enhances the performance of the group.

Both collaborative and cooperative learning practices involve active learning in smaller group settings.

CULTURALLY RESPONSIVE TEACHING is a pedagogy that recognizes the importance of including students' cultural background in all aspects of learning.

DATA (aka **FOOTPRINT OF LEARNING**) usually takes the form of a student portfolio with work collected over the course of a project, unit, semester, or class. A collection of LEOs can be seen as qualitative data.

DIFFERENTIATION refers to the adaptation of classroom learning to suit each student's individual needs, strengths, preferences, and pace by either splitting the class into small groups, giving individual learning activities, or otherwise modifying the material. It is a flexible system for students to achieve understanding at a point where they can do that.

JIGSAW is a learning method in which individuals within the group study different aspects or pieces of a topic, then come together to teach one another about what they have learned. The goal is to reinforce learning through dialogue and social interaction so that all can share the information. When using LEOs, each student focuses on one Learning Experience Organizer (a single puzzle piece) to inform the group. They then can come together to enrich the learning experience.

A **LENS** is a way to view/see/read things based on a particular focus or point of view.

A **LEARNING EXPERIENCE ORGANIZER (LEO)** is a term we're using to make the shift from "planning a lesson" to "designing an inquiry-driven learning experience." Tradition would have us call the tools in Chapter 5 "worksheets," "study guides," "role sheets," or even "graphic organizers." All these terms can be used, but we suggest the term Learning Experience Organizer because they are open-ended sheets designed for inquiry, choice, active-learning, and collaborative learning.

MULTIMODAL/MULTIMODALITY/MULTILITERACIES are terms used to create a more inclusive picture of literacy beyond print texts. These terms reinforce the idea that literacies are transferred across modalities (from print to screen to sounds). A multimodal classroom is one that utilizes the whole range of texts and literacies available to the learner. One of the best early articulations of these ideas comes from the New London Group's (1996) "A Pedagogy of Multiliteracies: Designing Social Futures."

A **SIGNIFICANT LEARNING EXPERIENCE** includes student engagement and a "high-energy" classroom level. The outcomes of such an experience should be "significant and lasting change" and "value in life." Significant learning should enhance one's life, help one to contribute to the community, and prepare one for the working world (Fink, 2003).

TEXT/MEDIA TEXT: A text—in the postmodern sense of the word—can be any print or nonprint object. Of course, a book is a text, but building on that, a TV show, a poster, a popular song, the latest fashion, a garden, or a building can also be a text. Each medium does have unique features, be it an infographic, a cartoon, a museum display, a beach, a rock video, a fairy tale, or a police drama. The unique features of each text are always powerful to discuss with students.

Paulo Freire expands the idea of the world as a text in his book *Literacy: Reading the Word and the World*. In it he says:

> Reading the world always precedes reading the word, and reading the word implies continually reading the world. As suggested earlier, this movement from the word to the world is always present; even the spoken word flows from our reading of the world. In a way, however, we can go further and say that reading the word is not preceded merely by reading the world, but by a certain form of writing it or rewriting it, that is, of transforming it by means of a conscious, practical work. For me, this dynamic movement is central to the literacy process. (2000, p. 35).

This exemplifies the extended view of text.

TRANSFERENCE—sometimes called "Transfer of Learning," "Knowledge/Skills Transfer," or in job contexts, "Transfer of Training"—refers to the application of skills, knowledge, and/or attitudes learned in one learning experience to another learning experience (Perkins & Salomon, 1994).

How People Learn by the National Academy of Sciences (2000) defines transfer as "the ability to extend what has been learned in one context to new contexts. Educators hope that students will transfer learning from one problem to another within a course, from one year in school to another, between school and home, and from school to workplace. Assumptions about transfer accompany the belief that it is better to broadly 'educate' people than simply 'train' them to perform particular tasks" (p. 51).

References and Resources

Introduction

Ball, D. L., & Cohen, D. K. (1996). Reform by the book: What is—or might be—the role of curriculum materials to teacher learning and instructional reform? *Educational Researcher, 25*(9), 6–8, 14.

Christel, M. T., & Hayes, S. (2010). Teaching multimodal/multimedia literacy. In E. Lindemann (Ed.), *Reading the past, writing the future: A century of American literacy education and the National Council of Teachers of English* (pp. 217–250). Urbana, IL: National Council of Teachers of English.

Cope, B., & Kalantzis, M. (Eds.). (2000). *Multiliteracies: Literacy learning and the design of social futures*. London: Routledge.

Daniels, H. (2002). *Literature circles: Voice and choice in book clubs and reading groups*. Portland, ME: Stenhouse.

Davis, E. A., & Krajcik, J. S. (2005). Designing educative curriculum materials to promote teacher learning. *Educational Researcher, 34*(3), 3–14.

Hobbs, R. (2007). *Reading the media: Media literacy in high school English*. New York: Teachers College Press.

Jenkins, H. (with Clinton, K., Purushotma, R., Robison, A. J., & Weigel, M.). (2006). *Confronting the challenges of participatory culture: Media education for the 21st Century*. An occasional paper on digital media and learning. Chicago: John D. and Catherine T. MacArthur Foundation.

Johnson, D. W., & Johnson, R. T. (1999). Making cooperative learning work. *Theory into Practice, 38*(2), 67–73.

Kagan, S., & Kagan, M. (2009). *Kagan Cooperative Learning:* San Clemente, CA: Kagan Cooperative Learning.

Kaiser Foundation. (2010). *Generation M2: Media in the lives of 8- to 18-year-olds*. Retrieved from kff.org/other/poll-finding/report-generation-m2-media-in-the-lives

Kirkland, D. E. (2013). *A search past silence: The literacy of young Black men*. New York: Teachers College Press.

Kist, W. (2004). *New literacies in action: Teaching and learning in multiple media*. New York: Teachers College Press.

Lakoff, G., & Johnson, M. (1980). *Metaphors we live by*. Chicago: University of Chicago Press.

Lincoln Center Education. (2015). *Capacities for imaginative thinking: LCE's approach to arts education*. Retrieved from lincolncentereducation.org/about#capacities-for-imaginative-thinking.

National Council for the Social Studies (NCSS). (2013). *The college, career, and civic life (C3) framework for social studies state standards: Guidance for enhancing the rigor of K–12 civics, economics, geography, and history*. Silver Spring, MD: NCSS. Retrieved from socialstudies.org/c3.

National Governors Association Center for Best Practices and Council of Chief State School Officers. (2010). *The common core state standards for English language arts & literacy in history/social studies, science, and technical subjects*. Washington, DC: National

Governors Association Center for Best Practices and Council of Chief State School Officers. Retrieved from corestandards.org/wp-content/uploads/ELA_Standards.pdf.

National Governors Association Center for Best Practices and Council of Chief State School Officers. (2010). *The common core state standards for mathematical practice.* Washington, DC: National Governors Association Center for Best Practices, Council of Chief State School Officers. Retrieved from corestandards.org/Math/Practice.

New London Group. (1996). A pedagogy of multiliteracies: Designing social futures. *Harvard Educational Review, 66*(1), 60–92.

New Media Consortium. (2011). *The NMC horizon report: 2011 K–12 edition.* Retrieved from redarchive.nmc.org/publications/horizon-report-2011-k-12-edition.

NGSS Lead States. (2013). *Next generation science standards: For states, by states.* Washington, DC: The National Academies Press.

Ritchhart, R., Church, M., & Morrison, K. (2011). *Making thinking visible: How to promote engagement, understanding, and independence for all learners.* San Francisco: Jossey-Bass.

Chapter 1

Alvermann, D. E., Bogdanich, J. L. (2015). "Now is the winter of our discontent": Shakespeare, Kuhn, and instability in the field of reading education. In R. J. Spiro, M. DeSchryver, M. S. Hagerman, P. M. Morsink, & P. Thompson (Eds.), *Reading at a crossroads? Disjunctures and continuities in current conceptions and practices* (pp. 129–138). New York: Routledge.

Armstrong, D. P., Patberg, J., & Dewitz, P. (1988). Reading guides—helping students understand. *Journal of Reading, 31*(6), 532–541.

Armstrong, T. (2009). *Multiple intelligences in the classroom.* Alexandria, VA: ASCD.

Ball, D. L., & Cohen, D. K. (1996). Reform by the book: What is—or might be—the role of curriculum materials to teacher learning and instructional reform? *Educational Researcher, 25*(9), 6–8, 14.

Bizar, M., & Daniels, H. (2005). *Teaching the best practice way: Methods that matter, k–12.* Portland, ME: Stenhouse.

Broughton, J. (2008). Inconvenient feet: How youth and popular culture meet resistance in education. In K. S. Sealey (Ed.), *Film, politics, and education: Cinematic pedagogy across the disciplines* (pp. 17–38). New York: Peter Lang.

Csikszentmihalyi, M. (1997). *Creativity: Flow and the psychology of discovery and invention.* New York: HarperPerennial.

Daniels. H. (1993). *Literature circles: Voice and choice in book clubs and reading groups.* Portland, ME: Stenhouse.

Daniels, H. (2006). What's the next big thing with literature circles? *Voices from the Middle 13*(4), 10–15.

Darling-Hammond, L., Barron, B., Pearson, D., & Schoenfeld. A. (2008). *Powerful learning: What we know about teaching for learning.* San Francisco, CA: Jossey-Bass.

Davis, E. A., & Krajcik, J. S. (2005). Designing educative curriculum materials to promote teacher learning. *Educational Researcher, 34*(3), 3–14.

Dweck, C. (2007). *Mindset: The new psychology of success.* New York: Ballantine Books.

Fink, D. (2003). *Creating significant learning experiences: An integrated approach to designing college courses.* San Francisco, CA: Jossey-Bass.

Fiske, J. (2010). *Reading the popular.* New York: Routledge.

Freire, P., & Macedo, D. (1987). *Literacy: Reading the word and the world.* South Hadley, MA: Bergen & Garvey Publishers.

Gardner, H. (1994). *Frames of mind: The theory of multiple intelligences.* New York: Basic Books.

Gay, G. (2010). *Culturally responsive teaching: Theory, research and practice.* New York, NY: Teachers College Press.

Hagood, M. C., Alvermann, D. E., & Heron-Hruby, A. (2010). *Bring it to class: Unpacking pop culture in literacy learning.* New York: Teachers College Press.

Hayes-Jacobs, H. (2006). *Active literacy across the curriculum.* Larchmont, NY: Eye On Education.

Hattie. J. (2011). *Visible learning for teachers: Maximizing impact on learning.* New York: Routledge.

Hattie, J., & Yates, G. C. R. (2013). *Visible learning and the science of how we learn.* New York: Routledge.

Heacox, D. (2012). *Differentiating instruction in the regular classroom: How to reach and teach all learners.* Minneapolis: Free Spirit Publishing.

John-Steiner, V. (2000). *Creative collaboration.* New York: Oxford University Press.

Kirkland, D. E. (2013). *A search past silence: The literacy of young Black men.* New York: Teachers College Press.

Kist, W. (2004). *New literacies in action: Teaching and learning in multiple media.* New York: Teachers College Press.

Lakoff, G., & Johnson, M. (1980). *Metaphors we live by.* Chicago: University of Chicago Press.

Marzano, R. J., Pickering, D. J., & Pollack, J. E. (2001). *Classroom instruction that works: Research-based strategies for increasing student achievement.* Alexandria, VA: ASCD.

Maxworthy, A. G. (1993). Do study guides improve text comprehension? *Reading Horizons, 34*(2), 137–150.

New London Group. (1996). A pedagogy of multiliteracies: Designing social futures. *Harvard Educational Review, 66*(1), 60–92.

Overbaugh, R. C., & Schultz, L. (n.d.). *Bloom's Taxonomy.* Retrieved from ww2.odu.edu/educ/roverbau/Bloom/blooms_taxonomy.htm

Perkins, D. N., & Salomon, G. (1994). Transfer of learning. In T. Husen & T. N. Postlethwaite (Eds.), *The international encyclopedia of education* (2nd ed., vol. 11, pp. 6452–6457). Oxford, UK: Pergamon Press.

Pink, D. H. (2009). *Drive: The surprising truth about what motivates us.* New York: Riverhead Books.

Pink, D. H. (2005). *A whole new mind: Why right-brainers will rule the future.* New York: Riverhead Books.

Ritchhart, R., Church, M., & Morrison, K. (2011). *Making thinking visible: How to promote engagement, understanding, and independence for all learners.* San Franciso: Jossey-Bass.

Silver, H. F., Strong, R. W., & Perini, M. J. (2000). *So each may learn: Integrating learning styles and multiple intelligences.* Alexandria, VA: ASCD.

Sinek, S. (2009, September). *How great leaders inspire action.* [Video file]. Retrieved from www.ted.com/talks/simon_sinek_how_great_leaders_inspire_action

Sinek, S. (2009). *Start with why: How great leaders inspire everyone to take action.* New York: Penguin.

Slavin, R. E. (1990). *Cooperative learning: Theory, research, and practice.* Englewood Cliffs, NJ: Prentice Hall.

Smith, A., Juzwik, M. M., & Cushman, E. (2015). (Dis)orienting spaces in literacy learning and teaching: Affects, ideologies, and textual objects. *Research in the Teaching of English, 49*(3), 193–199.

Tomlinson, C. A. (2014). *The differentiated classroom: Responding to the needs of all learners.* Alexandria, VA: ASCD

Tomlinson, C. A. (2003). *Fulfilling the promise of the differentiated classroom: Strategies and tools for responsive teaching.* Alexandria, VA: ASCD.

Vygotsky, L. S. (1978). *Mind in society: The development of higher psychological processes.* Cambridge, MA: Harvard University Press.

Wagner, T. (2008). *The global achievement gap: Why even our best schools don't teach the new survival skills our children need—and what we can do about it.* New York: Basic Books.

Wiggins, G., & McTighe, J. (2005). *Understanding by design.* Alexandria, VA: ASCD.

Wiske, M. S. (Ed.). (1998). *Teaching for understanding: Linking research with practice.* San Francisco, CA: Jossey-Bass.

Chapter 2

Alvermann, D. E., & Bogdanich, J. L. (2015). "Now is the winter of our discontent": Shakespeare, Kuhn, and instability in the field of reading education. In R. J. Spiro, M. DeSchryver, M. S. Hagerman, P. M. Morsink, & P. Thompson (Eds.), *Reading at a crossroads? Disjunctures and continuities in current conceptions and practices* (pp. 129–138). New York: Routledge.

Brothers, E. L., Gillan, L., Goldsmith-Thomas, E., Goldstein, J. (Producers), & Rozema, P. (Director). (2008). *Kit Kittredge: An American girl* [Motion picture]. United States: Picturehouse Films and New Line Cinema.

DeVito, D., Shamberg, M., & Sher, S. (Producers), & Niccol, A. (Director). (1997). *Gattaca* [Motion picture]. United States: Columbia Pictures.

Golding. W. (2003). *Lord of the flies.* New York: Perigree Books. (Original work published 1954)

Hattie, J., & Yates, G. C. R. (2013). *Visible learning and the science of how we learn.* New York: Routledge.

Kohn, A. (1993). *Punished by rewards: The trouble with gold stars, incentive plans, a's, praise, and other bribes.* Boston: Houghton Mifflin.

Lennon. J., & McCartney, P. (1968). Revolution. On *The Beatles* (*The White Album*) [LP]. London: Apple Records.

McLuhan, M. (2003). *Understanding media: The extensions of man.* Berkeley, CA: Gingko Press. (Original work published 1964)

Michaels, L. (Producer), & Waters, M. (Director). (2004). *Mean girls.* [Motion picture]. United States: Paramount.

Newall, G., Eisner, M. (Producers), & Warburton, T. (Director). (2002). *Schoolhouse rock!* (Special 30th anniversary ed.). [DVD]. United States: Walt Disney Studios Home Entertainment.

Spiegelman, A. (1986). *Maus I: A survivor's tale: my father bleeds history.* New York: Pantheon.

Springsteen, B. (2008). *The ghost of Tom Joad* [CD]. New York: Columbia Records.

Steinbeck, J. (1939). *The grapes of wrath.* New York: Viking Press.

Index

Acknowledgments

Both Ryan and Pam want to thank NCTE and Free Spirit Publishing for their enthusiastic support and encouragement. We particularly want to thank Judy Galbraith and Meg Bratsch at Free Spirit Publishing and Felice Kaufmann and Kurt Austin in NCTE's publications division for their insight, support, enthusiasm, and flexibility. We also want to thank the entire Free Spirit team, including the special contributions of Lauren Ernt, editors Margie Lisovskis and Darsi Dreyer, and the design team of Steven Hauge, Colleen Rollins, and Michelle Lee Lagerroos.

We also want to thank the following colleagues for their professional contributions and advice on the Chapter 4 resources: Frank Baker, Kelly Wood Farrow, Kristin Goble, William Kist, Sandhya Nankani, Nick Sousanis, and all the folks on the Making Curriculum Pop social network who responded to our queries when we were looking further afield.

We would also like to thank four people who made key contributions to the book: First we want to thank Bill Kist for his brilliant foreword. He captured our vision with his trademark intellect, elegance, and wit. Bill is a wonderful person and a giant in the field. We are honored to stand on his shoulders.

Blake Goble, web master and designer at the National Opinion Research Center (NORC) and movie reviewer at the *Consequence of Sound* website, for his Chapter 4 suggestions and editorial assistance on films.

Nicole Trackman, an English teacher at the Illinois Math and Science Academy, for her overall contributions as well as her coauthorship of the "Ways of Teaching Popular and Common Texts" section in Chapter 2.

Stefanie Geeve, a math teacher and instructional coach at Glenbard West High School, for her inspiration for two of our math LEOs: the X-cavator (name coined by Lisbeth Goble) and Information Designer.

From Pam: Thank you to all the students and teachers who shared their stories with me through the years. Without their thoughtful ideas about teaching and learning, this book would not have been possible. I particularly want to thank Maribeth Campbell, Nicole Dodendorf, Jessica Goble, Kristin Goble, Lisbeth Goble, Paula Hennessey, Sandy Lutz, Bobbi Minogue, Julie Robertson, Delaine Robinson, Jamie Schumacher, Susan Sparks, and Nicole Trackman—an amazing group of smart women who make life wonderful and fabulous. They read, think, listen, discuss, reflect, and are genuinely extraordinary. I feel blessed to know them and wish that everyone could be surrounded by their magic. Oh, and the best part: they make me laugh!

I also would like to thank my family, starting with my mom and dad for reading to me as a child and for making books, radio, TV, magazines, and movies a big part of our household. They were text-savvy parents, even then; they talked to me about anything and everything.

My husband, Roger, who "gets me." Everyone needs that person in his or her life. He has been the one.

My four children, and their spouses, for their belief that I can accomplish anything. I am a lucky mom. They are fun, funny, brilliant, kind, giving, and caring. I also thank my grandchildren for keeping me young.

Thanks to Ryan for his profound understanding of the importance of media and text and his choice of collaborator for this book.

From Ryan: I want to thank all the wacky and wonderful students and educators that I have had the joy of collaborating with over the years. There are likely too many to list, but interacting with some special folks has made for an amazing journey.

From Hitsville, U.S.A: Derek Thornton; at Huron High School: Arthur Williams and the entire IES crew, especially Paul "Big Rig" Baldoni, Greg Brown, Ali Hussain, Jared "Salty Dog" Saltiel, and co-teacher Jen Boylan Sessa; Cleveland peeps via the Rock and Roll Hall of Fame Museum—Steve Armstrong, David "Verbal Math" McCullough, and Santina Protopapa; at Barrington High School: Nick Gerger, Veronica Roth, and Mark Zieder; at TIDE: Laura Broderick, Kelly Farrow, David Krodel, Michele Schuler, Kimberley Stansbury, and Pamela Trilla-Guzior; at TC: Nick "Unflattening" Sousanis, Christina Shon, and Michelle "Piper" Dumont; at NYCDOE: the entire Banana Kelly crew, especially Joshua Laub, Stephanie Young, Napoleon Knight, Alexander Dvorak, Lauren Fardig, Elizabeth Davis, D.J. Jerome, Amanda Hunter, and Karl Boyno; at Maine West High School: Jane Wisdom (and her, ahem, better half, Chris Fiorillo); at *The New York Times* Learning Network: Katherine Schulten; at NASA-GISS NYC: Carolyn Harris and Pushker Kharecha; at Westmont CUSD 201: Nancy Bartoz, Kevin Carey, and Amy Quattrone; at Lyons Township High School: Scott Eggerding, Karen Raino, and the entire BECCI and Humanities teams; at CPS: The whole Fulton crew, especially Jose Anaya, Rodney Bly, Julie Iverson, Richard Jung Shonda Huery-Hardman, Christine Keller, Natalie Laino, and Lorenzo Russell; at Bolingbrook High School: Michele Albano; at Glenbard 87's central office: Dave Larson, Jeff "DJF" Feucht, Eliana Callan, Janet Cook, Patrick Donohue, Robert Lang, Rod Molek, and Jamie "Super Woman" Wilson; at the Glenbard 87 schools, all the amazing teachers I've had the chance to spend time with, as well as the talented leadership teams, including Joshua Chambers, John Mensik, Peter Monaghan, Sandra Coughlin, Lorie Cristofaro, Shahe Bagdasarian, John Healy, Rebecca Sulaver; the inspiring math department chairs David Elliot, Haresh Harpalani, Michele Hawbaker, and Robert Urbain; and the mindblowing instructional coaches cooperative that makes my work a joy, Sheri Alonso, Marisa Abrams, Stefanie Geeve, Kelly Hass, James Hultgren, Joe Kulesza, Jeremy Meisinger, Suzanne Paul-Giffey, Mike Roethler, Marti Seaton, and Carole Toombs.

At the NCTE Media Commission in all its iterations: Richard Beach, Belinha De Abreu, Renee Hobbs, Alan Teasley, Nathan Phillips, Cyndy Scheibe, Robyn Seglem, Antero Garcia, and all the brilliant minds I've met and collaborated with at the NCTE Media Commission meetings over the last twelve years who have not been mentioned in other places; at UM: the Fred Goodman crew, including Lynn Malinoff, Jeffrey Stanzler, Jeff Kupperman, and Remi Holden, as well as the formative folks along the way, Andy Cashman, Tim Fagan, Matt Maasdam, Seth "Sloth" and Kelly Konkey, Jeff Hodak, Warren Lockette, Andrew Rodgers, Camran Shafii, Rich Witt, Angelique Durham Zerillo. To you, I say #GoBl(u)e.

Also, the teachers who helped me read "the word and the world": at Stevenson High School: Mary Christel, Denise Foster, David Noskin, and—to quote my brother Blake— "many families have a family doctor; ours has a family coach." That would be the coach for all seasons, John Schauble; at the University of Michigan–Ann Arbor: Carolyn Balducci, Fred Goodman, and Andrea K. Henderson (now at UC–Irvine); at Columbia University– Teachers College: John Broughton, Renee Cherow-O'Leary (now of Education for the 21st Century), Maxine Greene, and Ruth Vinz.

All of these people have inspired, taught, and collaborated with me the last twenty-five years on this whole learning journey in profound and joyful ways.

Thank you to the most important members of our extended family, Jovita Harm, and her daughter Karina and husband Ed, for all that you have added to our household. Of course, special thanks to my brother and sisters for their wit, verve, and ideas, and to Rog and Pam for being great adventurers, collaborators, teachers, mentors, and parents.

Finally, thank you to my wife, Nicole, for her patience, wisdom, intelligence, and love. I'm looking forward to sharing the rest of my life with you and our wonderful daughter Téa as we "read the world" together.

About the Authors

Pam Goble, Ed.D., has been a middle school teacher for thirty years and has taught education, humanities, and literature courses as an adjunct professor for the past fifteen years. She has presented at numerous conferences, such as the National Council of Teachers of English and the Association for Middle Level Education, and at Columbia University's *Teach, Think, Play* workshops. She also worked with NASA scientists at Columbia University to develop an interdisciplinary curriculum on climate change for middle school. She has published in the *Journal of Staff Development* and has written a chapter in an upcoming text for college professors on writing for undergraduates. Pam specializes in interdisciplinary learning, gifted education, curriculum and instruction, leadership, literacy, humanities, and adult learning. She lives in Long Grove, Illinois, with her husband.

Ryan R. Goble, M.A., is the teaching and learning coordinator for Glenbard Township High School District 87 in Glen Ellyn, Illinois. He specializes in creating joyful, collaborative, and sustainable learning experiences that "pop" for learners of all ages in formal and informal settings. His career began as a high school English teacher in Ann Arbor, Michigan. Since then he has taught, consulted, and presented for a wide variety of students, teachers, schools, colleges, school districts, and educational organizations all over the United States, including the Rock and Roll Hall of Fame and Museum and NASA's Goddard Institute for Space Studies. His work has been featured in many places, including *Teacher Magazine*, *The Journal of Staff Development*, *The Boston Globe,* and *The New York Times* Learning Network.

Ryan also is the founder of the educational consulting company Mindblue.com, and he shares exciting resources with teachers all over the world through his online social network Making Curriculum Pop. Ryan holds a master's degree in education and a bachelor's degree in English from the University of Michigan. He is also a doctoral candidate in interdisciplinary studies at Teachers College, Columbia University. He lives in Aurora, Illinois, with his wife and daughter.

Other Great Resources from Free Spirit

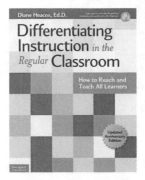

Differentiating Instruction in the Regular Classroom
How to Reach and Teach All Learners (Updated Anniversary Edition)
by Diane Heacox, Ed.D.
For teachers and administrators, K–12.
176 pp.; paperback; 8½" x 11"; includes digital content

Making Differentiation a Habit
How to Ensure Success in Academically Diverse Classrooms
by Diane Heacox, Ed.D.
For teachers and administrators, grades K–12.
192 pp.; paperback; 8½" x 11"; includes digital content

Advancing Differentiation
Thinking and Learning for the 21st Century
by Richard M. Cash, Ed.D.
For K–12 teachers and adminstrators.
208 pp.; paperback; 8½" x 11"; includes digital content

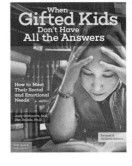

Differentiation for Gifted Learners
Going Beyond the Basics
by Diane Heacox, Ed.D., and Richard M. Cash, Ed.D.
For K–12 teachers, gifted education teachers, program directors, administrators, instructional coaches, curriculum developers.
224 pp.; paperback; 8½" x 11"; includes digital content

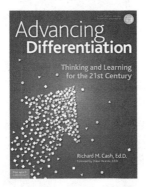

The Common Sense Guide to the Common Core
Teacher-Tested Tools for Implementation
Katherine McKnight, Ph.D.
For K–12 teachers, administrators, district leaders, curriculum directors, coaches, PLCs, preservice teachers, university professors.
240 pp.; paperback; 8½" x 11"; includes digital content

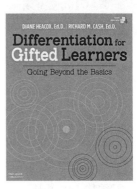

When Gifted Kids Don't Have All the Answers
How to Meet Their Social and Emotional Needs (Revised and Updated Edition)
by Judy Galbraith, M.A., and Jim Delisle, Ph.D.
For Teachers, gifted coordinators, guidance counselors, and parents of gifted children, K–9.
288 pp.; paperback; 7¼" x 9¼"; includes digital content

Teaching Smarter
An Unconventional Guide to Boosting Student Success
by Patrick Kelley, M.A.
For middle school and high school teachers.
208 pp.; paperback; 7¼" x 9¼"; includes digital content

They Broke the Law—You Be the Judge
True Cases of Teen Crime
by Thomas A. Jacobs, J.D.
For ages 12 & up.
224 pp.; paperback; 6" x 9"

Interested in purchasing multiple quantities and receiving volume disounts?
Contact edsales@freespirit.com or call 1.800.735.7323 and ask for Education Sales.

Many Free Spirit authors are available for speaking engagements, workshops, and keynotes.
Contact speakers@freespirit.com or call 1.800.735.7323.

For pricing information, to place an order, or to request a free catalog, contact:

Free Spirit Publishing Inc. • 6325 Sandburg Road • Suite 100 • Golden Valley, MN 55427-3629
toll-free 800.735.7323 • local 612.338.2068 • fax 612.337.5050
help4kids@freespirit.com • www.freespirit.com